ODD ANGLES OF HEAVEN
Contemporary Poetry by People of Faith

To Stan and Delores –
More words in response to
the Word – And thank you for another
year of reaching into the dark, for
your beautiful examples of self-
giving.

Love,
Jan & Louis
Christmas 1994

ODD
ANGLES
—OF—
HEAVEN

CONTEMPORARY
POETRY
BY PEOPLE
OF FAITH

DAVID CRAIG &
JANET McCANN
EDITORS

Harold Shaw Publishers
Wheaton, Illinois

Edition copyright © 1994 by David Craig and Janet McCann

Rights to individual poems retained by the poets and/or their publishers.

Edited and introduced by David Craig and Janet McCann

ISBN 0-87788-614-8

Library of Congress Cataloging-in-Publication Data

Odd angles of heaven : contemporary poetry by people of faith / edited
  and introduced by David Craig and Janet McCann.
      p.   cm.
    ISBN 0-87788-614-8 (pbk.)
    1. Religious poetry, American. 2. American poetry—20th century.
  I. Craig, David, 1951-   . II. McCann, Janet.
  PS595.R4034 1994
  811'.54080382—dc20   93-47065
                                                           CIP

---

99 98 97 96 95 94

10 9 8 7 6 5 4 3 2 1

CONTENTS

Acknowledgments

We thank all the publishers and poets who have donated reprint
and publishing fees to the alleviation of world hunger.
—the editors

Paul Allen: "The Man with the Hardest Belly" first appeared in *Ontario Review*, Spring-Summer 1989 and is reprinted by permission of the poet.

Tom Andrews: "Praying with George Herbert in Late Winter" first appeared in *Poetry*, © 1992 The Modern Poetry Association, 60 W. Walton St., Chicago, IL 60610, and is reprinted by permission of the Editor of *Poetry*. It is part of *The Hemophiliac's Motorcycle*, © 1994 by Tom Andrews and is reprinted by permission of University of Iowa Press, 119 West Park Road, 100 Kuhl House, Iowa City, IA 52242-1000. "Song of a Country Priest" from *The Brother's Country*, © 1990 by Tom Andrews is reprinted by permission of Persea Books, 60 Madison Avenue, New York, NY 10010.

Jackie Bartley: "The Convent" first appeared in *the eleventh MUSE*, Winter 1991-92, Volume 10, Number 2 and is reprinted by permission of the poet. "Confirmation" first appeared in *West Branch* 31/32 and is reprinted by permission of the poet.

Jill Peláez Baumgaertner: "Bilbao Alone" first appeared in *First Things*, 156 5th Ave., New York, NY 10010 and is reprinted by permission of the editor. "For Sophie, Bald in Church" first appeared in *Ariel* and is reprinted by permission of the poet.

Bruce Bawer: "Art and Worship" first appeared in *The American Scholar* and is reprinted by permission of the poet.

Wendell Berry: "To What Listens," "The Way of Pain," "Desolation," "The Law That Marries All Things," "The River Bridged and Forgot" from *Collected Poems 1957–1982*. Copyright © 1984 by Wendell Berry. Reprinted by permission of North Point Press, a division of Farrar, Straus & Giroux, Inc., 19 Union Square West, New York, NY 10003.

James Bertolino: "How Could I Have Doubted?" is reprinted by permission of the poet.

Fr. Murray Bodo OFM: "To Francis of Assisi" first appeared in *Franciscan Life* and is reprinted by permission of the poet. "Teresa of Avila" first appeared in *St. Anthony Messenger* and is reprinted by permission of the poet. "Oscar Romero" first appeared in *Clifton Magazine* and is reprinted by permission of the poet.

Scott Cairns: "The Theology of Delight" and "On Slow Learning" from *The Theology of Doubt* © 1985 by Scott Cairns. Reprinted by permission of the poet and Cleveland State University Poetry Center, Cleveland State University, 1983 E. 24th St., Cleveland, OH 44115. "On Slow Learning" first appeared in *Jeopardy Magazine*. "Yellow" and "Infirmities" from *The Translation of Babel*, © 1990 by Scott Cairns is reprinted by permission of The University of Georgia Press, 330 Research Dr., Suite B-100, Athens, GA 30602-2760. "Yellow" first appeared in *Zone 3*. "Murmur" from *Figures for the Ghost* by Scott Cairns is reprinted by permission of The University of Georgia Press, 330 Research Dr., Suite B-100, Athens, GA 30602-2760.

Turner Cassity: "Carpenters" from *Steeplejacks in Babel*, reprinted by permission of the poet and David R. Godine, Horticultural Hall, 300 Massachusetts Ave., Boston, MA 02115.

Sybil Estess: "Villa de Matel" is reprinted by permission of the poet.

Robert A. Fink: "On Jesus, Taking His Word on Immortality" and "My Sons Ask Where God Lives" first appeared in *Michigan Quarterly Review* 22 (1983): 377 ("My Sons . . .") and 378 ("On Jesus . . ."). "Foot Reflexologist, Farmers and Christmas" first appeared in *Triquarterly* 68 (Winter 1987): 86-87, Northwestern University. All poems are also included in *The Ghostly Hitchhiker*, © 1989 by Robert A. Fink, Corona Publishing's Poetry Series, 1037 South Alamo, San Antonio, TX 78210. Reprinted by permission of Corona Publishing Company.

John Finlay: "The Bog Sacrifice" from *Mind and Blood: The Collected Poems of John Finlay*, © by John Finlay, John Daniel Press, P.O. Box 21922, Santa Barbara, CA 93121 is reprinted by permission of his literary executor.

Nola Garrett: "Job, Too" first appeared in *The Georgia Review*, Winter 1989, Vol. XLIII, No. 4 and is reprinted by permission of the poet.

Dana Gioia: "Guide to the Other Gallery" is reprinted by permission of the poet. "All Souls'" from *The Gods of Winter* (Graywolf Press, St. Paul, MN), © 1991 by Dana Gioia, is reprinted by permission of the poet. "The Burning Ladder" and "Instructions for the Afternoon" from *Daily Horoscope* (Graywolf Press, St. Paul, MN), © 1986 by Dana Gioia, are reprinted by permission of the poet.

Diane Glancy: "Light Beneath the Skin (or Pronoun 2)," "The Transformation Band," and "Theology of Deer" are reprinted by permission of the poet.

Jorie Graham: "Noli Me Tangere" and "Breakdancing" from *The End of Beauty*, © 1987 by Jorie Graham (The Ecco Press).

James Hoggard: "Improvisation Before the Introit" first appeared in *The Hampden-Sydney Poetry Review* and is reprinted by permission of the poet.

John R. Holmes: "Solvite Templum Hoc" first appeared in *The Cord*, Vol. 38, No. 5, May 1988, p. 159, Drawer F., St. Bonaventure, NY 14778 and is reprinted by permission of the editor.

David Brendan Hopes: "Georges de la Tour: *The Penitent Magdalene* circa 1640," "A Passion Play," "Jumping Jack" are reprinted by permission of the poet. "*The Penitent Magdalene*" first appeared in *Hiram Poetry Review*, Franciscan University Press. "A Passion Play" first appeared in *Mid-American Review*, Franciscan University Press.

Andrew Hudgins: "The Cestello Annunciation," "Heat Lightning in a Time of Drought," "Christ As a Gardener" from *The Never-Ending*, © 1991 by Andrew Hudgins. Reprinted by permission of Houghton Mifflin Company. All rights reserved. "The Cestello Annunciation" is reprinted by permission from *The Hudson Review*, Vol. XLIII, No. 1 (Spring 1990). Copyright © 1990 by Andrew Hudgins. "Heat Lightning in a Time of Drought" first appeared in *The Georgia Review*.

Jean Janzen: "Identifying the Fire" first appeared in *POETRY*, August 1991, and was copyrighted in 1991 by The Modern Poetry Association and reprinted by permission of the editor of *POETRY*, 60 W. Walton St., Chicago, IL 60610. "Facets" received the Roberts Writing Award 1990 and is reprinted by permission of the poet. "Plain Wedding" first appeared in *Gettysburg Review*, Spring 1989 and is reprinted by permission of the poet and editors. It also appeared in *The Upside-Down Tree*, © 1992 by Jean Janzen and is reprinted by permission of the poet and Windflower Communications/Brandt Family Enterprises, 67 Flett Avenue, Winnipeg, Manitoba R2K 3N3 Canada. "Flowers of Amsterdam" has appeared in *Quarry West* and is reprinted by permission of the poet and editor. It also appeared in *The Upside-Down Tree*, © 1992 by Jean Janzen, and is reprinted by permission of Windflower Communications/Brandt Family Enterprises, 67 Flett Avenue, Winnipeg, Manitoba R2K 3N3 Canada.

Mark Jarman: "Ascension of the Red Madonna" from *The Rote Walker*, © 1981 by Mark Jarman (Carnegie Mellon University Press), is reprinted by permission of the poet. "Last Suppers" first appeared in *Shenandoah*, Winter 1991 and is reprinted by permission of the poet.

William Jolliff: "Loving Is the Worst of Christian Weather" first appeared in *Cincinnati Poetry Review* and is reprinted by permission of the poet.

Barbara Jordan: "We All Have Many Chances" and "The Cannibals of Autumn" from *Channel*, © 1990 by Barbara Jordan, is reprinted by permission of Beacon Press, 25 Beacon Street, Boston, MA 02108.

X. J. Kennedy: "The Waterbury Cross" from *Dark Horses: New Poems*, © 1993 by X. J. Kennedy, is reprinted by permission of The Johns Hopkins University Press, 2715 N. Charles Street, Baltimore, MD 21218-4319.

Jane Kenyon: "Twilight: After Haying" and "Things" © 1986 by Jane Kenyon. Reprinted from *The Boat of Quiet Hours* with the permission of Graywolf Press, Saint Paul, Minnesota. "Staying at Grandma's" and "While We Were Arguing" © 1990 by Jane Kenyon. Reprinted from *Let Evening Come* with the permission of Graywolf Press, Saint Paul, Minnesota.

Leonard Kress: "Shotputters and Discus Throwers" and "Mennonite Hills in Central Pennsylvania" are reprinted by permission of the poet.

Peter LaSalle: "What He Is Missing," "Ciudad Acuña," and "East Austin" are reprinted by permission of the poet. "Ciudad Acuña" first appeared in *Hampden-Sydney Poetry Review*. "East Austin" first appeared in *Illuminations* (U.K.).

Sydney Lea: "Prayer for the Little City" is reprinted with permission of Charles Scribner's Sons, an imprint of Macmillan Publishing Company, from *Prayer for the Little City*, © 1991 by Sydney Lea. "Road Agent" appeared in *The Blainville Testament*, a collection of narrative poems published by Story-Line Press, Three Oaks Farm, Brownsville, OR 97327 and is reprinted by permission of the editor. "Midway" first appeared in *The Atlantic*, April 1985 and in *No Sign*, © 1987 by Sydney Lea (The University of Georgia Press) and is reprinted by permission of the poet.

J. T. Ledbetter: "Gethsemani Abbey, Kentucky (remembering)" first appeared in *The Cresset*, Vol. LII, No. 3, January 1989.

Denise Levertov: "The Tide," "On a Theme by Thomas Merton," "Salvator Mundi: Via Crucis," "Contraband," "Ascension" from *Evening Train*, © 1992 by Denise Levertov. Reprinted by permission of New Directions Publishing Corp., 80 Eighth Avenue, New York, NY 10011.

Bob Lietz: "Before the Monstrance" first appeared in *Images* and is reprinted by permission of the poet. "Retreat" first appeared in *Cincinnati Poetry Review*. "River Road" is soon to be published in *Storm Service* by BasFal Books.

Marjorie Maddox: "Weeknights at the Cathedral" first appeared in *A Widening Light: Poems of the Incarnation*, edited by Luci Shaw, Harold Shaw Publishers, 1985 and is reprinted by permission of the poet. "Even the Rocks Shall Praise Him" first appeared in *The Louisville Review* and is reprinted by permission of the poet. "Threading the Needle" first appeared in *Kansas Quarterly* and is reprinted by permission of the poet.

Paul Mariani: "The Great Wheel" first appeared in *Image*, 4, Fall 1993 and is reprinted by permission of the poet. "Manhattan" first appeared in *New England Review*, 14.4, Fall 1992 and is reprinted by permission of the poet.

Janet McCann: "Logic" first appeared in *Whiskey Island*. It was published by Franciscan University Press in *Afterword* and is reprinted by permission of the poet.

Howard McCord: "A Letter of Saint Andrew the Dancer" from *Fables and Transfigurations*, © 1968 by Howard McCord, Kayak Books, San Francisco, 1968, is reprinted by permission of the poet.

Walter McDonald: "Faith Is a Radical Master" first appeared in *North Dakota Quarterly*, University of North Dakota, Box 8237, University Station, Grand Forks, ND 58202 and is reprinted by permission of the poet and editor. "Settling the Plains" from *Night Landings*, © 1989 by Walter

MacDonald. Reprinted by permission of HarperCollins Publishers, Inc., 10 East 53rd Street, New York, NY 10022. "Settling the Plans" was first published in the *Sewanee Review*, Vol. 97, No. 1, Winter 1989, University of the South, 735 University Avenue, Sewanee, TN 37375-1000 and is reprinted by permission of the editor. "Nearing the End of a Century" first appeared in *Soundings East* and is reprinted by permission of the poet.

David Middleton: "The Old Man's Flowers" and "Lines for the Dormition of the Virgin" are reprinted by permission of Louisiana State University Press, Louisiana State University, Baton Rouge, LA 70893. "Azaleas in Epiphany" is printed by permission of the poet.

Raymond Oliver: "The Pleasure Principle" first appeared in *Southern Humanities Review*, Spring 1974 and is reprinted by permission of the poet. "Compline" and "Christendom" are reprinted by permission of the poet. "Scripture Lesson" first appeared in *Entries* and is reprinted by permission of David R. Godine, Horticultural Hall, 300 Massachusetts Ave., Boston, MA 02115. "Seventeenth-Century Gravestone for a Child" appeared in *Triquarterly* and also in *Other Times*, a chapbook published by John Barth and is reprinted by permission of the poet.

Molly Peacock: "Prairie Prayer" first appeared in *Southwest Review* and is reprinted by permission of the poet.

Marjorie Power: "To an Atheist in a Spiritual Crisis" is reprinted by permission of the poet.

Wyatt Prunty: "The Taking Down" and "Blood" from *The Run of the House*, © 1993 by Wyatt Prunty. Reprinted by permission of the poet and the publisher, The Johns Hopkins University Press, 2715 N. Charles Street, Baltimore, MD 21218-4319.

Sister Bernetta Quinn: "Buddhist Temple on New Year's Day" is reprinted by permission of the poet.

Len Roberts: "My Brother's Angel" and "Clear January, zero degrees, my last" (the latter first published in *Now This*) are reprinted by permission of the poet. "When the Bishop Came" from *Black Wings* by Len Roberts. Copyright © 1989 by Len Roberts, reprinted by permission of Persea Books.

Mark Rozema: "Adrift" first appeared in *The Rolling Coulter*, Messiah College, Grantham, PA 17027 and is reprinted by permission of the editor. áThe Nuns of Vorkuta Prison" first appeared in *The New Mexico Humanities Review* and is reprinted by permission of the poet.

Larry Rubin: "Passing Over: Easter Dawn" first appeared in *Christianity and Literature*, Spring 1991 and is reprinted by permission of the poet. "Christmas Poem" from *Lanced In Light*, copyright © 1967 by Larry Rubin, reprinted by permission of Harcourt Brace & Company. "Early Easter" was first published by David R. Godine and is reprinted by permission of the poet.

Nicholas Samaras: "Flying to the Body of Christ" first appeared in *Journal of Ideology* and is reprinted by permission of the poet. "Words for Golgotha" and "Vespers" are reprinted by permission of the poet. "Movable Feasts" first appeared in *The Harvard Review* and is reprinted by permission of the poet.

Luci Shaw: "St. Frideswide's Chapel, Christ Church, Oxford" and "Golden Delicious" first appeared in *South Coast Poetry Journal*, English Dept., California State University, Fullerton, CA 92634 and is reprinted by permission of the editor. "Camping in the Cascades" is reprinted by permission of the poet.

Margaret D. Smith: "Moon" and "In a dry season" are reprinted by permission of the poet.

William Stafford: "Today" from *Stories and Storms and Strangers* (Honeybrook Press), © 1984 by William Stafford, is reprinted by permission of the poet. "Being Sorry," "At Summer Camp," "Listening at Little Lake Elkhart," and "At a Small College" from *A Scripture of Leaves*, © 1989 by William Stafford are reprinted by permission of Brethren Press, 1451 Dundee Avenue, Elgin, IL 60120-1694.

VISION, FAITH, POETRY

Janet McCann

Many believe that the post-Christian age has arrived. This is an era of posts; for some critics, post-post-modernism has now supplanted post-modernism. And on a gray Monday, one wonders: Can it be true that Christianity is no longer an active force in the intellectual world? After all, noted literary critic Helen Vendler claims that it is the lack of the spiritual that characterizes literature of this time; she even suggests that our literature draws its power from this void, its meaning informed by our awareness of ultimate meaninglessness. In the introduction to *The Harvard Book of Contemporary Poetry*, Vendler states that "There is no significant poet whose work does not mirror, both formally and in its preoccupations, the absence of the transcendent." I read this statement and picture today's poets as thousands of clockwork beetles, running around with briefcases, eyes riveted to the ground, expecting abysses to open beneath their feet. The Great Absence: Is this our new metaphor for the creative imagination, replacing both the mirror and the lamp?

Certainly cynicism abounds. But I find that it is shot through with questioning, a negativity interrogating itself. "I'm glad," a professor friend said, "that we had the kids baptized before we quit the church." A confusing assertion! Certainly the current academic scene is decentered, deconstructed, and virtually disemboweled, a perfect setting for moral ambiguity and self-destructing manifestos. The tools that we used twenty years ago are outdated and unacceptable, and the concept of literature itself has been so radically revised that we can barely recognize it. Literature is considered suspect by some, a privileging and enshrinement of less enlightened eras' biased value systems. What can we assert, we who think of ourselves as Christian poets and scholars? What can we say and expect to have received, not only by our colleagues who believe as we do but by the larger community?

"I'm glad," my friend said. Of what is he glad, I wondered. Does he see without admitting it some revitalization of an old system, a new generation rediscovering the truth of what he had for whatever reason discarded? Can we actively reread Christianity, finding the truth in it that can be present only in this new time? Christianity is not a closed system, like Aristotelian logic. It reflects its believers, the river of its life one in which you cannot step twice and find it the same water, the same place, the same banks. It is not the Church but the current of its life in its late twentieth-century members, we who are marked by our time period, who may be reading Thomas Aquinas and Derrida on CD-Rom and announcing choir rehearsals by E-mail. A series of images came to the mind of this female Christian poet, outdated and somewhat decentered, as my professor friend spoke: an old man and a grand-child, he telling her a story he doesn't think he believes any longer but hopes she will. A bank of flowers, an old wicker stroller, a curious new face. Water, from a fountain sparkling upward, statuary. Water flowing over a cupped hand, phospho-rescent. A burnt-out hulk of a building, a church. Next to it, a new one being built, experimental blocks of concrete, a whole wall of glass looking out on a field of flowers grown wild: larkspur, dogwood, hollyhocks. A huge cross of some glimmering new substance, just discovered . . . images of faith transforming form, welling in unex-pected places.

What did my friend the cynic rejoice in? Did something in him see the Church change and grow, shuck off the shells of congealed thought that bind it to the particulars of other times and ages, renew itself and clarify its force? Other famous naysayers have seen this. Wallace Stevens must have done so when, dying, he requested and received baptism as a Roman Catholic. As a young man rejecting his childhood faith, he must have held something in reserve: metaphorically baptized the children. And they grew up, and returned later to claim him.

There is no question that issues of faith and of the crisis of faith are of major importance in contemporary literature. For some writers it is a case of post-existen-tialism, as they look beyond the Sartrean fields of nihilism for stirrings of life. For many contemporary poets, this is a scene of waiting and listening. There is doubt and faith, and a whole spectrum of commitment. Some contemporary poets lose their faith to find it. The fluid of it is too much for the container; it flows around for a while, seeking, finds another. Others remain stable in their belief, poetry closer and closer to its ineffable center. In claiming that this is the post-Christian age, critics are paying too much attention to the surface, too little to what is growing underneath.

Of course, as always, there are directions or trends in Christian poetry. I don't like to assign poets to categories; the pigeonholed justly protest. Anyway, no one belongs exclusively to one group. Even when one categorizes historically, there are gaps and overlaps—metaphysicals writing cavalier poetry, and vice versa. So if I throw some names around, I mean only that some of the things these poets have written seem to fit into a category. And the groups themselves are protean, with no more definition than amoebas.

Some contemporary Christian poets see the world as Graham Greene did, as a violent foreign landscape where all the old signals are disconnected and we guide ourselves by their memory, as we might pore over a torn and outdated map which is, however, our guide for getting out of here. In this world of cataclysm, everything seems to mean something else, but Meaning itself remains: hard, immutable, and just beyond the grasp of understanding. This kind of Christianity is frightening. The possibility of sudden grace remains, a vertical abyss, terrifying. The poems are a call to rebirth, but a sense that the old self must shatter before this new emergence provides a feeling of threat. Elements of this perspective can clearly be seen in T. S. Eliot, in the poetry up to his breakdown. This is in fact a poetry of breakdown, of leaning over the edge. I might call these poets Cataclystics, and if their poems are often alarming and dizzying, they break through the veneer of comfort that often is a detriment to renewal or even to serious thought. Some of William Everson's work fits in here, and John Finlay's. Their challenge disturbs and disorients.

Another group is more nature-oriented, seeing in images of nature signs and images of God's presence. These poems are often energy-pent, as Gerard Manley Hopkins' are: "The world is charged with the grandeur of God . . ." This work is like that of the romantics, except that the natural surroundings reflect back not the self but God. These poets might be thought of as Luminists, as their poems glitter and glimmer with immanent light. To the natural light of the external world is added the inner light of the Christian visionary, often so subtly that the work comes across as strangely electric nature poetry. Amy Clampett and May Sarton come to mind, but this group is large. Their vision comforts and enlightens.

Contemporary poets also write directly about theology and divinity, either from a personal or a more abstract perspective. There are dark-night poems and poems of epiphany from those who are comfortable with the difficult material of spiritual quest. It takes courage as well as conviction to confront these issues. Often the influence of Donne, Crashaw, Vaughan, and Herbert is visible, although the surface of the poem is contemporary. These modern metaphysicals may use traditional forms to express the various stages of their spiritual investigations and their discoveries. Richard Wilbur, William Stafford, Dana Gioia, and many others have created compelling and honest quest poems.

Other general directions: Christianity may be represented in the context of a particular culture, bound with the other elements of a way of life: Catholic-ethnic; Protestant-ethnic. Louise Erdrich's work may be considered here, as well as X. J. Kennedy's, Stuart Dybek's, and others'. The poems in this group are also often in the nature category as well. Christianity may be seen as a vehicle for social action. Erdrich again, and Denise Levertov. These are often poems about Christian action that do not preach. Christian exegesis can be seen in William Stafford's poems and elsewhere. What I think of as Zen Christian poetry is work which merges Eastern meditative practice, and often a Haiku sensitivity to the tiniest of natural facts, with Christian belief. David Craig and Robert A. Fink may be considered here. Formalist meditative poems, often sonnets, provide the traditional pleasure of the form. Richard Wilbur, John Holmes, Vassar Miller, and many other current poets explore traditional rhyme and meter. On the other edge of form, experimentalists weave long narrative loops into mixed-form poems that provide a New Critic's delight of apparent surface chaos that resolves into underlying harmony. Paul Christensen's wordplay comes to mind here as well as that of Sidney Lea.

The spectrum of Christian poetry on the American literary scene today is broad, and much Christianity glimmers in the poetry that is not expressly Christian. As we come to the end of the twentieth century we experience the sense of endings, of fin-de-siecle jadedness and the feeling that everything has been written and done, but we know also the stirrings of rebirth. It is perhaps time for a new sort of post-post-modernism. We need more positive prefixes, re-, pre-, neo-, theo- to replace un-, post-. It is time to dismantle the chaos. Christian vision is both compatible with tradition and inventive, forthright and flexible. One would not go so far as to turn Vendler around and claim that there is no important work being done now that does not mirror the presence of the transcendent. But one could say that the variety and strength of religious poetry being written today demonstrates that the need for the sacred is as potent a force as ever, and its pure flame takes many shapes.

THE POWER
IN CHRISTIAN
POETRY

David Craig

*C*hristian poetry is a field not yet completely turned. It has, I think, more possibilities than the average Pelagian verse one sees today because it begins in the heart of possibility. It does not find its root in our muted selves or in some formless, directionless unconscious, but in the Maker of heaven and earth, the One who brought all things into being, through his Son, by means of the Holy Spirit. Every Christian has been saved by him; we owe our lives to him. And when we acknowledge that fact, either implicitly or explicitly, and seek only him, he gives life back again—bigger, broader, more abundantly.

This is the mercy of God: "a burst of joyful generosity." It is the holiness he gives to us, calls us to. That holiness can come surging through to the surface in poetry, by-passing the rational mind in a joyful spasm of surrealism, or it can come quietly, meditatively, full of questions, doubts, apprehensions, carrying with it all the sorrow in Adam's loins. Since the Comforter lives at our innermost place, it is he who enlivens our speech, language. Unlike deep image poets, Christians know who it is that pushes our work effusively up, moving furniture in the process, giving direction and scope to our delight, our pain. We can offer more than brief epiphany; our poems, like the medieval mystery plays did, like the Modernists tried to do, can offer history and meaning. We know who Jesus is, and what he has done, what he will do. We can never repay. And so, Christian poetry is thankful.

But Christian poetry is more than just that. Because we have been given abundant life, the faith our words embody can have a deeper effect. As we move toward him, we learn more and more clearly the redemptive value of suffering, how it can help heal the yawning wounds of that mystical body on the cross. How that, too, is good. We can also see the price we pay in our own individual lives as sin, our bane, gives way much too slowly. And yet, because he is in us, its grip lessens as we go. We work out our personal salvations with fear and trembling, and know, and can more deeply feel each day the price we pay for our little denials, our fears, which we cling to like idols. We feel a little of the hell in those denials, perhaps begin to realize, too, the horror of a hell that is not just in this life. And so our poetry consistently leads us to prayer.

As they say in the Christian East: "Christ is risen! Truly, he is risen!" He works all things to the good for those that love him. And despite the more than 20,000,000 dead innocents heaped into abortion mill garbage cans these past twenty or so years, despite the circus, the cynicism in Washington, despite what appears to be a Big Sister situation in the media, he is on his throne. So we who are called Christian, in the face of all this, act and wait. We know whom we serve.

Idolatry today is the norm. We can even see that within the writing community itself. But unlike so much of what is being written these days, the Christian poet does not need to make an idol of the imagination. Enjoy it, yes. Celebrate it, certainly. But we know it cannot save us. What saves us is our ultimate subject matter. Imagination is only the vehicle. He is reality; his, the only purely objective and life-giving vision. And, paradoxically, we know that the closer we allow ourselves to be drawn to him, the more fully human our perspectives become. We get closer to being who we were made to be; we get closer to Eden through our Savior, what he has done, who he is. We get closer to right relation. That's where the freedom is. That is where all the power and joy we can experience is. And how else could that joy possibly be better expressed than in and through poetry? Think of how much grace would be poured out on the world if there were 1,000 Francises, pens in hand!

But it is not power, in and of itself, we seek. True spirituality is about giving up personal power; it is in the political realm where one seeks to gain it. We, as Christians, seek firstly God's will. And that is a peaceful place, a place where we are free to mine the depths of wisdom as no other writers perhaps can. There is no end point, where we can go no further. We are free to grow in peace and wisdom and personal discipline until we stop asking for that growth. Our poetry can only deepen as we move closer to the love of Jesus, closer to the wound in his side, closer to the crown on his head. We can move forward in the power of the crucifixion, resurrection. And as our surrender becomes more complete, it becomes clearer why he says what he says: "My yoke is easy and my burden light." Here is the mercy of God. Both for ourselves and for others.

And lastly, there is family for us. A spiritual family. We have a wealth of friends to draw from—as you will find in these poems (though I do not profess to speak for all of the poets represented here)—a wealth of examples, exhorters, both in this life and from the next. Others have gone before. We, like they, are here "to kneel where prayer has been valid." To kneel and to dance. With tiny sunlit steps. In the streets or around the ark if we feel so moved. What Whitman so beautifully imagined: an illumined, eschatological procession, we are called to walk in daily. Each of us called, step by step, to sanctity, perfect holiness. Away from "the undisciplined squads of emotion," the sputterings of ambition; away from the new/old Pelagian view of human nature with its comfortable lie, its rational whitewash; away from skewed views of sexuality which can only serve to pull us from the Truth, Who is the Holy and does not change. He is where true power is. Our part is merely to say "yes," then stay out of his way. If we are truly meek, he will show up in our work; in power, yes, but even more than that, in our changing lives.

The Man with the Hardest Belly

Paul Allen

I

THE MAN WITH THE HARDEST BELLY knows God
compensates his loss of limbs—legs
to knee, nub arms—with a gift
to titillate the congregations when he is delivered
from Ocala in his motor home to call us to Christ.
This handsome chunk of what was left
after he'd been shucked, he says, at 14
found God by serving himself on our tables
if we had canned corn at all in 19 and 55.

We are not members here. As Dad said, we
have our own faith. But someone spirit-filled
made Mother promise. So we're here cross-legged
on the cool ground at the river,
and my father is chosen. The Youth Director
is chosen. The man high up in Amway
is chosen. The three of them hang
THE MAN WITH THE HARDEST BELLY over the first branch
of the maple like a sandbag on the levee.
He pops his torso, flips, chins
to the next branch, flips, grabs a limb
with his thighs. Left nub for leverage,
he hooks another V with the back
of his head, walks on stumps up the trunk
to the next limb, flips to his belly, bends,
flips, holds with his teeth. He maneuvers
like something stained and mating

1

toward the top of our slide in godless biology,
or like the little dots we see inside our own eyes
on days we're morose. The thing
we've come to watch we can't watch
directly as he works toward the sun. The higher
he goes, the more we must look down to save
our eyes. We pull grass, look up and squint
to check his progress, kill an ant climbing our shoe.
Some stand to change the angle,
to keep him closer to the shaded cars.
Settling high, balanced and swaying, he preaches
from the texts painted on his motor home
under the faded "DOUBT AND DELIVERY."

II

... *so look with me now at Genesis, whole people, Genesis 15:1-6. Abram. Abram
was a cripple in bed, had no standing among men. Listen to me, had no standing
among men, praise God, and Moses, who said no, not me, not me, God gave
Moses what he needed. And Joshua at their first real trial? Joshua didn't think he
could do nothing. Joshua 7:1-10. I thank God my arms and legs went to your soft
tummies in '55. I was born again in that shucking machine, look at my belly, my
hard and strong belly, you could park a truck on my belly praise God, God gives
you what you need. I need a strong belly and a lithe neck to climb trees and show
you the Holy Spirit at work, and show you the compensations of our precious
Lord. Praise you, Lord. The Holy Spirit turns my pages for me. Look at Joshua
splashing dirt up in his face. I'm here to tell you people there's no dirt in my face,
no Lord. And Gideon. It's right there in your book. Judges 6:1-14. What does God
say to that worthless garment of feces? (Excuse me, ladies, but the compensations
of God is nothing to be delicate about). Says to Gideon, go in your power. Go in
your power. Listen to me now: Go in your power and save my people. Read it.
Isn't that what it says? Your power. Don't look at me, I know I'm pretty. Look at
your book, look at your own Holy Word. Now examine, if you will, First*

2

Corinthians 10:13. See? God won't give you nothing wrong without a
correlational power to get out of it. . . . Jesus himself, his wonderment self, take
this cup from my lips, listen now, take this cup from my lips, take this cup. . . .

III

We pull off the road to let the other cars by.
The Youth Director finds a wide place.
And the man high up in Amway finds a wide place.
The three of us wait, our hazard lights blinking,
while the born again wave and the kids shout
from their windows that Jesus is the One
and fathers honk (Honk If You Love Jesus).
My father nods occasionally. My sister starts
it. We are arguing about whether
THE MAN WITH THE HARDEST BELLY crawls on all
four nubs around the rooms of his scriptural
motor home, or slithers like something run over.
Crawls. Slithers. My father hushes us. My sister hits
me, says, "For unto you is born *a child.*" I hit
my sister: "Let the women keep silent
in the Chevrolet." My mother has had enough.
She separates us. We aren't to speak. We aren't
to utter a peep. Each of us must look out our own window.

IV

The cars are thinning. We can hear the hazards now.
The road is dark and the dust is settling.
"I told her we'd go, and we went," my mother says.
"I told you we'd come, and we came," my father says.

3

"I thought it a bit much, though," she says, "when
he stood on his perch, spread those arms
and screamed, 'Nail me. Nail me.' "
"Me too," my father says, "nails wouldn't work."
My mother is looking at him. He says,
"Toggle bolts might work."
"Go help him down," my mother says, "and let's go home."

My father joins the other two on the road. They walk
back toward the river. My mother tells us it will
turn cool; we don't need to bathe when we get home,
but we do need to wash our feet. My father appears.
He eases us between the Youth Director and the man
high up in Amway. When we're on the main road
and the others have turned off, my mother says,
"I thought we'd have your mother over tomorrow.
Remind me to get a ham out when we get home."
"And corn?" my father says. "Whatever," she says.

V

Tonight down the cold upstairs hall we hear
them laughing, my mother and father.
Tonight we hear them making love again.

Praying with George Herbert in Late Winter

Tom Andrews

1.

In fits and starts, Lord,
    our words work
the other side of language

where you lie if you can be said
    to lie. Mercy upon
the priest who calls on you

to nurture and to terrorize
    him, for you oblige.
Mercy upon you, breath's engine

returning what is to what is.
    Outside, light swarms
and particularizes the snow;

tree limbs crack with ice
    and drop. I can say
there is a larger something

inside me. I can say,
    "Gratitude is
a strange country." But what

would I give to live there?

2.

Something breaks in us,
and keeps breaking. Charity,
      be severe with me.
Mercy, lay on your hands.

White robes on
the cypress tree. Sparrows
      clot the fence posts;
they hop once and weave

      through the bleached air.
Lord, I drift on the words
      I speak to you—
the words take on

      and utter me. In what
language are you not
      what *we* say you are?
Surprise me, Lord, as a seed

      surprises itself . . .

3.

Today the sun has the inward look
of the eye of the Christ Child.
    Grace falls at odd angles from heaven

    to earth: my sins are bright sparks
in the dark of blamelessness . . .
    Yes. From my window I watch a boy step

backwards down the snow-covered road,
studying his sudden boot tracks.
   The wedding of his look and the world!

   And for a moment, Lord, I think
I understand about you and silence . . .
   But what a racket I make in telling you.

Song of a Country Priest

"Naturally I keep my thoughts to myself."
—*Bernanos*, Diary of a Country Priest

April 4. Wind hums
in the fireweed, the dogwood
drops white skirts across

the lawn. From this window
I've watched the pink shimmer
of morning light spread

to the sky and the blond
grass lift the dew. *You*
in whose yet greater light,

etc. My prayers grow
smaller each dawn. Each dawn
I wake to this landscape

of thyme, rue, a maple
whose roots are the highways
of ants, cattails down

to the river. I rise
and look and learn again:
I believe in my backyard.

I can mimic the sway
of weeds in wind. I can
study the patience

of tendrils. God knows what
I am, a rib of earth?
a hidden cloud? I am

old now. I am a priest
without believers. I counsel
leaves, fallen petals, two

bluejays and one shy wren.
In my book of Genesis,
the serpent says, "You can't

tempt me with green
peppers, yellow squash,
the ripe meats of Eden.

I'm looking under my
belly for the next meal.
I'm lying beside a dirt

road in West Virginia,
waiting for a pickup
to stir a thick cloud

of dust into my mouth.
I will never hunger.
I will live like this

forever—inching with
rhythm across the dried
dirt, pulling myself

like a white glove through
meal after parched, ecstatic
meal . . ."

Perhaps my blasphemies
have saved me. Perhaps God
reads between these lines,

that whiteness touched
by no one. I'm ready
for Him to settle my

body like an argument;
my ashes can settle
where they will. God could

fall like an evening sun
to say Eat dust
with the serpent, crawl

on your belly. He could
say the earth is a secret
told by quartz vein and

nothing else. Tonight
in the thin dark He could
whisper the sky is the

earth, the stars are foxgloves,
quince blossoms, white flames
of trilliums, and I am

flaring and vanishing
above them. I'm ready.
I would believe it all.

The Convent

Jackie Bartley

You must learn first
what is hardest,
give yourself over
each morning, leave
whomever you thought
you were
behind, on the pillow.

In time this parting
will seem natural.
You will become
transparent, candlelight
will pass through you.

Then you are ready
to swallow the silence,
dark as a cave,
a hollow that encloses
even the smallest task.

Your hands will know
the days by heart
and hold them
on a toothbrush
in a dust rag, around a loaf
of bread, on every bead
of your Rosary.

You will store your prayers
in clothesbaskets
and kitchen drawers.

Confirmation

Sometimes
on the verge
of sleep, I hear
my name whispered
in a small voice
that is neither
male nor female,
that neither seeks
to counsel nor
be counseled.

I've been told
that only our name,
spoken with reverence
or with need
can wake us this peaceably,
as if its quiet abbreviation
of our being
echoes from some crevice
in the past,
reverberates from the smooth
black surface of the future.

It may be that, in that moment,
a friend whose thoughts
lay elsewhere
suddenly seeks us out,
or an ancient ancestor,
some lost soul,
disconnects in time
and slips into a space
that we've left vacant.

But sometimes when it comes
it is so faint, it passes
so quickly,
I've barely time to wake
with *yes*
on my lips.

Bilbao Alone

Jill Peláez Baumgaertner

Some of the sounds here are familiar:
Vivaldi plays the same in this language,
keys rattle in locks,

the engines of buses sigh as they turn street corners.
But something is different,
an odd solitude.

It digs itself under my watch into the small bones
of my wrist. Here in this place are no extras.
I play the leading role, but I am

as anonymous as my skeleton.
I have no drawers of envelopes and paper here,
no cupboards of glasses turned neatly upside down,

no simmering stews, no one whose knees fit
perfectly behind mine as I sleep.
Nothing of myself is here except myself.

What I have extends over vast landscapes
and it requires me to do nothing.
I sit in a park and watch what passes:

short Basque men whose tobacco lingers long after they
have gone, dogs whose interest is each other,
workmen with a ladder, the dignified bus

driver before the return trip, hands crossed behind.
And then suddenly it is twilight.
Sometimes one watches for no reason other than the eyes.

Is this grace, this waiting, a simple existing inside of it?
Is it always as ominous as these first few
hours of unfamiliarity?

For Sophie, Bald in Church

The others on whom cancer
also closes in wear wigs or scarves
but your head is bare

and smooth as a peach.
You wear it cleanly
and there is no Auschwitz

agony in your eyes although
you also know that other type of
baldness sour and silent. But now you

ask about what happens later—
if the soul hovers in the out there
floating in dreams waiting

for the body to catch up.
And we in our habitual pews
sit behind you and see the cross

through the penumbra of your
head—naked as an infant
still curling into its mother.

Art and Worship

"But Bruce, why can't you worship Art?"
—*H.Z.*

Bruce Bawer

However it may help us to transcend
or comprehend this vast, impermanent
realm where we commingle and contend,
furnishing us, as it were, with wings,
art is a means of worship, not an end,
the way we formulate, share, and present
to the far-off and unfathomed firmament
the yearnings of our souls toward higher things.

If a sculpture, story, symphony,
or some stray strain played on a violin
seems to articulate a verity
resoundingly, it is because it springs
out of a kindred sensibility,
soaring above the universal din
to remind us all that we are kin
with anyone whom song inspires to sing.

And yet there is an all-surpassing thrill
toward which the highest art can only tend
as circumstance, facility, and will,
and all divine endowment will allow;
the more immaculately to distill,
with every small degree it may ascend,
that which is eternally beyond,
and which we humbly ponder and avow.

To glorify a man, or venerate
his works, is therefore racial vanity;
revering art, we falsely elevate
ourselves, and fail to see that, here below
the height, our art is to articulate
that which we witness only partially,
finding forms for what we know must be,
yet can't be understood by what we know.

To What Listens

Wendell Berry

I come to it again
and again, the thought of the wren
opening his song here
to no human ear—
no woman to look up,
no man to turn his head.
The farm will sink then
from all we have done and said.
Beauty will lie, fold
on fold, upon it. Foreseeing
it so, I cannot withhold
love. But from the height
and distance of foresight,
how well I like it
as it is! The river shining,
the bare trees on the bank,
the house set snug
as a stone in the hill's flank,
the pasture behind it green.
Its songs and loves throb
in my head till like the wren
I sing—to what listens—again.

The Way of Pain

1.

For parents, the only way
is hard. We who give life
give pain. There is no help.
Yet we who give pain
give love; by pain we learn
the extremity of love.

2.

I read of Abraham's sacrifice
the Voice required of him,
so that he led to the altar
and the knife his only son.
The beloved life was spared
that time, but not the pain.
It was the pain that was required.

3.

I read of Christ crucified,
the only begotten Son
sacrificed to flesh and time
and all our woe. He died
and rose, but who does not tremble
for his pain, his loneliness,
and the darkness of the sixth hour?

21

Unless we grieve like Mary
at His grave, giving Him up
as lost, no Easter morning comes.

4.

And then I slept, and dreamed
the life of my only son
was required of me, and I
must bring him to the edge
of pain, not knowing why.
I woke, and yet that pain
was true. It brought his life
to the full in me. I bore him
suffering, with love like the sun,
too bright, unsparing, whole.

Desolation

A gracious Spirit sings as it comes
and goes. It moves forever
among things. Earth and flesh, passing
into each other, sing together.

Turned against that song, we go
where no singing is or light
or need coupled with its yes,
but spite, despair, fear, and loneliness.

Unless the solitary will forbear,
time enters the flesh to sever
passion from all care,
annul the lineage of consequence.

Unless the solitary will forbear,
the blade enters the ground
to tear the world's comfort
out, root and crown.

The Law That Marries All Things

1.

The cloud is free only
to go with the wind.

The rain is free
only in falling.

The water is free only
in its gathering together,

in its downward courses,
in its rising into air.

2.

In law is rest
if you love the law,
if you enter, singing, into it
as water in its descent.

3.

Or song is truest law,
and you must enter singing;
it has no other entrance.

It is the great chorus
of parts. The only outlawry
is in division.

4.

Whatever is singing
is found, awaiting the return
of whatever is lost.

5.

Meet us in the air
over the water,
sing the swallows.

Meet me, meet me,
the redbird sings,
here here hcre here.

The River Bridged and Forgot

Who can impair thee, mighty King

Bridged and forgot, the river
in unwearying descent
carries down the soil
of ravaged uplands, waste
and acid from the strip mines,
poisons of our false
prosperity. What mind
regains of clarity
mourns, the current a slow
cortege of everything
that we have given up,
the materials of Creation
wrecked, the strewed substance
of our trust and dignity.

But on still afternoons
of summer, the water's face
recovers clouds, the shapes
of leaves. Maple, willow,
sycamore stand light
and easy in their weight,
their branching forms formed
on the water, and yellow
warbler, swallow, oriole
stroke their deft flight
through the river's serene reflection
of the sky, as though, corrupted,
it shows the incorrupt.
Is this memory or promise?

26

And what is grief beside it?
What is anger beside it?
It is unfinished. It will not
be finished. And a man's life
will be, although his work
will not, nor his desire
for clarity. Beside
this dark passage of water
I make my work, lifework
of many lives that has
no end, for it takes circles
of years, of birth and death
for pattern, eternal form
visible in mystery.
It takes for pattern the heavenly
and earthly song of which
it is a part, which holds it
from despair: the joined voices
of all things, all muteness
vocal in their harmony.
For that, though none can hear
or sing it all, though I
must by nature fail,
my work has turned away
the priced infinity
of mechanical desire.

This work that many loves
inspire teaches the mind
resemblance to the earth
in seasonal fashioning,
departures and returns
of song. The hands strive
against their gravity
for envisioned lights and forms,

fallings of harmony;
they strive, fail at their season's
end. The seasonless river
lays hand and handiwork
upon the world, obedient
to a greater Mind, whole
past holding or beholding,
in whose flexing signature
all the dooms assemble
and become the lives of things.

How Could I Have Doubted?

James Bertolino

It was second grade, a parochial
school, and I was new in town, new with
my many-voweled name and dark complexion.
That Spring, after all the kids had turned seven,
we would have the Lord's chalky wafer
placed on our tongues.

The nun who taught us was the one we thought
was blonde—Sister Mary Benjamin—but like the others,
she was careful never to show her hair. We thrilled
to rumors of a Summer camp where sisters went free
of their white and black, where hair rippled when they swam,
and bare legs were warmed by sun.

For months she prepared us for that grave
and brilliant Sunday, when we would join the endless
procession of the guilty. She told us that on the grand
morning of membership in the Mystical Body of Christ,
the Lord would smile on each of us, and for that moment
could deny nothing requested by these brave and

glowing children. What power we were given!
I knew and knew what my wish would be—I needed
to become the *real* Superman. If only I could fly, and see
through walls and clothing, hear what whispers
were kept from me, and have the strength of Samson,
then I knew I'd be loved and happy.

It wouldn't matter that my head was flat, ears
like Dumbo's, and my bicycle older than any
on the playground. They would all see how important
I knew I was. I thought of little else for weeks, rehearsing
the six easy words: Dear   God   Please
Make   Me   Superman.

Some of the others wondered what I
would ask, and told of toys or fishing gear
or dresses, but I held my secret. They would know
when I could show them. I saw myself rising into
the air, host still dissolving on my tongue, and turning
toward the congregation with face illumined,

simple smile saying: "how could you have doubted?"
Finally the day came, and I knelt at the communion
rail. The priest, with his altar boy, moved mouth
by mouth toward me. I saw the white disks on
tongue after tongue, and my heart raced, waiting
for the power to touch me.

I repeated my request, my demand, with each step, each
rustle of the vestments: Superman, Superman, Superman.
Soon that consecrated hand withdrew my own first host
from the chalice. It made a tiny sign of the cross,
then moved so slowly toward my face. Sudden panic.
Fear. God will strike me dead!

What if asking this is blasphemy?
For several endless seconds, while the paper-dry
wafer bonded to my tongue, I struggled with
the horror of my plan. In a rush of relief I whispered
"Dear God, please give me three dollars
and twenty-five cents."

It was a beginning. I knew I would never
be the same. Sad I lacked the resolve to grasp
my dream, but happy I had survived my first confrontation
with the divine. By early afternoon I'd received
three cards from relatives and friends, each offering
a single dollar bill. As I stepped

out of the house onto the sun-dappled
porch, on my way to the Sunday matinee,
Mother called after me: "Here, honey,
here's some money for candy,"
and God handed me
a quarter.

To Francis of Assisi

Fr. Murray Bodo OFM

I feel you floating down,
descending from Subasio's crest
like Icarus into his waiting sea.

But you fall toward lepers'
open arms, wolves' hungry jaws.
With them you laugh at the heights

you fell from. Your descent is
ascent to Love who fell
into the Virgin Mary's womb.

Like Christ's, your coming down,
down-coming, rises heavenward.
Poverty's not without wings.

It lifts. And we who live below
rise by going farther down with Him
who fell that we might fly

with poor, bruised hands and feet.
We soar in lepers' skins, we praise
from wolves' and beggars' mouths.

Teresa of Avila

If you say to this mountain, "Be lifted from your place and hurled into the sea," and have no doubts, but believe that what you say is happening, it will be done for you.
—*Mark 11:23*

The road from Toledo to Avila:
the feel of sagebrush and cactus
where olive and pine like giant
broccoli grow.

Stone castles look like adobe
pueblos and you go up and up
through rock and mountain
barren but for poppies and broom
sweeping you higher to incongruous
beds of lavender.

This altitude dizzies but does not
purify. This climb is outside
to the high city of Avila, not
the climb inside, up the mountain
soul becomes when you try to
move it into the sea,

move it or climb it or enter its
narrow cleft that widens through
cool adobe tunnels into a crystal
cave, an interior castle.

Oscar Romero

When they sing the funeral Mass for Oscar Romero
there isn't room for all the campesinos
in the church. Many stand outside. Like Moses
they take off their shoes for the Compañero,
the Breaker of Bread, who lies there broken, too.
The soldiers come sprinkling lead,
the shower breaks the ranks of worshippers.
When they silence their deadly aspergils
there are bodies and pocks of bullets
in the walls, as usual, and—filed like
rows of witnesses—the empty shoes.

The Theology of Delight

Scott Cairns

Imagine a world, this ridiculous,
tentative thing blooming
in your hand. There in your hand, a world
opening up, stretching, after the image
of your hand. Imagine
a field of sheep grazing, or a single sheep
grazing and wandering in the delight
of grass, of flowers
lifting themselves, after their fashion,
to be flowers. Or a woman, lifting her hand
to touch her brow, and the intricacy
of the motion that frees her
to set the flat part of her hand
carelessly to her brow. Once,
while walking, I came across a woman
whose walking had brought her
to a shaded spot near a field.
Enjoying that cool place together,
we sat watching sheep and the wind
moving the small flowers in the field.
As we rose to set out again, our movement
startled the flock into running; they ran
only a little way before settling again
into their blank consideration
of the grass. But one of them continued,
its prancing taking it far into the field
where, free of the others, it leapt for

no clear reason, and set out walking
through a gathering of flowers, parting
that grip of flowers with its face.

Yellow

The town is much larger than you recall,
but you can still recognize the poor:
they vote to lose every chance they get, their faces
carry the tattoo of past embarrassments,

they are altogether too careful. This girl,
here in the print dress, pretending to shop
for an extravagance, the too slow way
her hand lingers between the colors along

the rack, her tentative hold on the clasp—
sure signs she knows she has no business here.
Soon enough she'll go home again with nothing
especially new in her hand, but no one

needs to rush things. The afternoon itself
is unhurried, and the lighted air outside
the store has lilacs in it. Her hand finds
a yellow dress. I think she should try it on.

Infirmities

Some mornings, you know you've seen
things like this before.
The kind woman across the street
is lame, and her daughter is lame.

Some defect they've had since birth
is working to dissolve their bones.
The boy three doors down
is blind. And the idiot
girl who sweeps up at the market
insists all day on her own
strange tune. And sometimes they seem
happy enough and sometimes
you might find one alone, muffling
grief with a coat sleeve.

And the shy way the blind boy
laughs when he stumbles
makes you laugh with him some mornings.
Some mornings it hurts to see.

On Slow Learning

If you've ever owned
a tortoise, you know
how terribly difficult
paper training can be
for some pets.

Even if you get so far
as to instill in your tortoise
the value of achieving the paper,
there remains one obstacle—
your tortoise's intrinsic sloth.

Even a well-intentioned tortoise
may find himself in his journeys
to be painfully far from the mark.

Failing, your tortoise may shy away
for weeks within his shell, utterly ashamed,
or, looking up with tiny, wet eyes, might offer
an honest shrug. Forgive him.

Murmur

God Stammers with Us . . .
—Calvin

What is this familiar pulse beginning
in the throat which promises to pronounce
for once the heart's severer expectations
but which will not be articulated
from the glib, unhelpful mass of the tongue?

Late winter, the chill can go either way—
brief renewal, habitual decay.
Against our shore the sea extends again
its unrelenting question, and withdraws.
In such weather, the little boats stay put.

And who can blame them? This uncertainty
is the constant weather our horizon
employs to keep our expeditions brief
and—to the point—ineffectual,
while all the while the cliffs beneath us fail.

Still, the murmur of what the heart would like
to say, and saying to attain, repeats
our trouble: these little ventures with the tongue
are doomed by their very mode of travel.
The limits become what we cannot bear.

Carpenters

Turner Cassity

Forgiven, unforgiven, they who drive the nails
    Know what they do: they hammer.
  If they doubt, if their vocation fails,
    They only swell the number,

Large already, of the mutineers and thieves.
    With only chance and duty
  There to cloak them, they elect and nail.
    The vinegar will pity.

Judas who sops, their silver his accuser, errs
    To blame the unrewarded.
  They guard the branch he hangs from. Guilt occurs
    Where it can be afforded.

In the Garden by the Sea: Easter

Kelly Cherry

These giant grape hyacinths
Rise like porticoes from stems like plinths,
Flinging their fragrance

On the April air.
Something *is* everywhere,
Something like air

Or God, is there where you thought
There was nothing, not
Anything, where matter, caught

And stuck
On a hook,
Squirms and is eaten, solider than any book

A writer ever wrote.
Something exists that is not merely of note,
Something unwritten but wrought

In sense and dimension,
Something like an ocean,
Say, or the moment of bright tension

Before the body gives
Itself to the idea that it lives
And is loved and loves and grieves

For the incommunicant,
Whom nothing touches
And something can't.

Gethsemane

On a hill backlit by twilight,
the disciples gather like crows
for the night.

This is their down time, time to browse
among the olive branches, Christ with them,
their apostolic flight slowed at last to a head-nodding drowse,

to a flutter of tattered cloak, the unraveling hem
dragging in the dirt like a hurt wing.
They flock momentarily around him,

then settle down, safe in the soft swing
of wind that rises and then falls back
with the deepening evening

into the distance, and sleep, while Christ's black
feathers burn in his father's fist,
plucked by God before by Judas kissed.

Galilee

Suppose another time while walking on water
he grew weary and decided to sit down
upon a wave cresting in a white curve
under the sun, to catch his breath, and fish
swam back and forth around him, silver needles
sewing the sea in a seamless stitchery,
the sun a sequin on the bright bodice of sky,
the anchoring hem of his robe embroidered with salt.

You on the shore! Can you imagine how
you would have felt, knowing that here was a god
at sea, one who had already gotten
his feet wet, one who, though he was not in
over his head, was drifting even then
toward the nakedness of eternity?

Song about the Second Creation

Like a stone, sound drops
into being; the waters part,
the waters close; the waves fan out, unfurled.
This is the second creation—not the bone's bright light
that starts and stops, having merely beckoned,
but the one eternity echoes,
love—the sung word flung into the world by God's loud hand.

Reading, Dreaming, Hiding

"You asked me what is the good of reading the Gospels in Greek."
—*Czeslaw Milosz, "Readings"*

You were reading. I was dreaming
The color blue. The wind was hiding
In the trees and rain was streaming
Down the window, full of darkness.

Rain was dreaming in the trees. You
Were full of darkness. The wind was streaming
Down the window, the color blue.
I was reading and hiding.

The wind was full of darkness and rain
Was streaming in the trees and down the window.
The color blue was full of darkness, dreaming
In the wind and trees. I was reading you.

I'll Fly Away

Michael Chitwood

There's a snag in the oak.
A dust of snow reveals the harvest stubble
as lines on a page
and they are only rows of harvest stubble.
There's the red fruit of the holly
and the cedar's blue.
There's the glitter of the moon on ice
and it's only glitter.
There's a snag in the oak
I can't get by.

*

Rodney said he wouldn't go.
I said I wouldn't.
Wendell said he would and was gone
from the back pew
to where the reformed Hindu, now evangelist, wept
because his mother and father died
Hindu and he would never see them
on the Shores of Glory.
I went.

*

Can God make a door so small
he can't get through it?
Can he do anything?

There was only the moon
in its cold path, straight and narrow.

     *

Beggar's-lice on my knees keep asking for the field.
I believe what they believe.
I believe in the thistle at the right hand,
the mortal rip,
the salt of the body.

This Is the Day the Lord Has Made

"I'll have no truck with angels,"
he says to his stunned boots,
sole up by the silage cutter.
The snapped drive chain writhes
in the dust of his field.
His ring finger wears his ring
and one rusted link of the chain.
"No truck," he says into his chest pocket.
His watch pays no heed.
The dust gets up and does a jig.
His lonesome finger scratches an itch.
He thinks he'll just lay back a little.
A cross hangs on a thermal, a hawk
hauling its keen hunger into heaven.

Let My People Go

Sublime: To transform directly from the solid to the gaseous state.

Naphthalene sublimes at room temperature.
The room, for instance, where he said
"Other women, name one,"
the room where she said "No, never"
and shut each cupboard,
the room they brought him into
and did not shut his eyes
and the men outside wiped the sides
of their boots on the grass and waited.
Naphthalene sublimes.

A white crystalline compound, C10H8,
derived from coal tar,
each fossil
steps out onto the normal air
like Jesus hiking over the gunnel,
holding up, just a little, the hem of this robe.

O Naphthalene, I would house like you
in the cedar chest, in the fragrant gate of going away.
I would be useful too,
as a moth repellent, as an explosive.

Naphthalene saves.
I have seen it in neon
and believe those bones.
I have seen the old man dance
the Saint Vitus,
his progress down the street,
his slick hair and worn shoes.

Naphthalene sublimes. Hallelujah.
We are His people, a throng in the noon.
Naphthalene sublimes. Glory be to the Deliverer.
He comes to the gate
and all who go out
will be like the dust of the road,
will rise up.

A Prayer

Paul Christensen

I'm out there somewhere, wandering around
under the street lights. I can hear my own
foot steps coming through the wall.
It is raining out; the cars are like
griddle plates frying some mysterious
supper of birds and moonlight. There are
men gathered at the counter reading
the bible, smoking cigarettes. The coffee
is hot and sour, and leaves a rank
smell of burning leaves on their breath.

My loneliness rises like a winter sun,
and there are paths that have frozen
under the morning ice. No one is looking
for me. I am sealed behind the landscape,
in a corner of the daylight where nothing
is possible. There, soul-like and silent
as time, I wait, leaning on the shadow
of God, which has built up a pillow of
grit and dust in the mind. This is the
stranger who lurks in me, whom I reach
out to like some desperate child, begging
to be answered by this prayer.

Answer me, answer the door, any door, let
him in and call me when he comes. He's
wearing a blue shirt and thrift-store shoes,
he's out of touch. What you offer you give
to yourself. But you knew that. You knew

all along this was the word aching to
touch your tongue, to ride the nerves
out of your own darkness into love.

The Fathers

David Citino

My children can't wait to leave
this town, their friends' fathers
home all week month after month
and dressed for Saturday,
getting in the way of child's play
and lusting after the wife
the moment she comes in from work,
mowing the lawn a week before it's time,
waxing the car until it gives them back
every worry line of one graying face.
The company moved to the sun,
or forced them into give-backs
until there was nothing to do
but strike, or laid them off
so long ago they no longer figure
in the unemployment rate
because benefits have run out.
They've quit looking, quit shaving,
quit counting the beers.
Even the dentists are up late
going over and over the books.
All my life I've lived among them,
Cleveland, Akron and Marion,
Youngstown, Toledo and Detroit
shrinking one neighborhood at a time,
roads south loaded with rental trucks
and pickups. Now their mills are cold,
machine shops boarded up, warehouses
rented out to artists and entrepreneurs,

mothballed ore boats secure
at river moorings, railroad tracks
stained blood-orange
with rust's rough patina.
To save money, St. Mary's
no longer rings the Angelus bells.
Three times each day I hear the silence.

The Pastor's Creed

Michelangelo's dead wrong. Adam had no navel.
He was born unattached.

Frogs come spontaneously from Nile mud. A woman and man
can burst into flame for no reason at all.

Swans, silent all their lives, sing like the devil
when Death splashes toward them. So should we.

Lemmings are the wisest of creatures, most realistic.
Bees die of sorrow to learn they've caused hurt.
Wolves lust after the flesh of young brides.

Teeth, nails and hair ignore the reaper, grow
till Judgment Day. Quicklime in time
returns all beauty to dust. A body falling
from a many storied height's dead before it touches earth.

Because they're gotten with a greater enthusiasm,
bastards make better artists, lovers, priests, saviors.

God striped the melon to make it easier for father
to cut it into equal slices.

Unwary women can get into trouble in bath water,
during dreams, in the stable, before any mirror.

Drinking from a garden hose fills the belly
with snakes. Birth hurts. Love. Death. God made
Eve's pelvis narrow enough to squeeze her children's heads,
to teach them life's a series of constraints;
narrow enough to pleasure Adam in the night, to give him

57

a preview of paradise. When an old woman falls
her pelvis shatters, to illustrate the gravity of age.

Wars are good for religion, religion for wars.

This life of desperation soon must end. Thus we must learn
to rejoice, to mourn.

There are more extinct than living species.
More corpses than lovers.

Sister Mary Appassionata Delivers an Impromptu Speech at the Local Ponderosa

Go right ahead. Gorge beasts
on grain, and feed in turn
on beasts. Nine of every ten
calories involved, *you lose.*

Hindus say 330,000,000 gods
in the body of each cow.
In India alone, 180,000,000 cows.
Go figure how many that makes,

each mad as hell about some sin,
venial or mortal, a bureaucrat
insisting His or Her version
Is, Was, and *Forever Shall,*

whining over calendar or tithe.
No way you'll please them all.
What's there to do to live
the good life but do without?

The Talmud claims the demons
in this world number 7,495,926,
bellies fat with sin, barely
enough to go around N Y C,

much less gird the globe.
Surely we're underestimating
the enemy's troop strength.
Thank God an unhungry angel

walks with each of us.
We've a holy war on our hands.
Pigs get hungry enough,
they'll eat anything—

one another even. But go
to the Jains, who seal up bugs
by the millions in temple rooms
amid enormous cornucopias

of the sweetest treats,
until each has come to know
that sated, eternal sleep.
Such holy care not to disturb

tick or mealy worm or grub,
tread on dust or put out
even the merest life,
the way to light, O love !

Sister Mary Appassionata Lectures the Science Class:
Fossils, Physics, Apple, Heart

Fossil bones, splintered bits of pelvis,
jawbone, tooth and skull aren't
of early apes and men
but of fallen angels made by greed too gross
to fly, who shattered when they hit the ground.

We know from physics every clock
winds down, each woman and man lies down
one more time than necessary for sleep or love.
Every movement culminates in stone,
each light and life in the ocean of night.

Drowned bodies, drunkards, heroes, saviors
surface always on the third day.

Virgin wool cures the deepest ache or burn.

Girls with big breasts and too much heart won't
fit into heaven. The boy who can unclasp
a girl's brassiere with one hand
knows too much for his own good
and all his life will have his hands full,
his mouth open at the wrong time.

The key to happiness? Knowing every second
of every day what to do with the hands,
when to loose or hold the tongue.

The holiest creatures are those that fly. God
Himself's part falcon, cuckoo, pelican, dove.

The girl who indulges herself
by climbing spiked fences, riding a horse
with too much passion, stooping too often
to pick mushroom or orchid
or dreaming of lovers who feel as she does
will from the wedding night on
be too easy on her husband.

Man's the only animal dumb enough to try
to cry back the dead, take
another's life only out of spite,
give his life for love.

Those whose eyebrows meet can never be trusted.

Women named Agnes always go mad.

No hunger justifies eating an apple
without first bringing it to life by breathing
on it, filling it with beauty
by rubbing it across the heart.

Madrigal

Peter Cooley

It is always the same poem.
It should begin *O hear me Lord O*
and then music could dispense with all the words
and the euphony of speechlessness would praise for me.
But in practice that cannot come to pass.
There must be some theme like a catalpa tree this evening
lowering, adagio, the wind among its limbs
outside a kitchen window where the timpani of dinner plates resounds
as set down by a tired woman. There must be her husband splashing wine.
into two glasses reflecting the oven's plucked brown wings
where juices hum their promise of largesse.
There must be words spoken by one or both which grate and clash
before the children who choose this moment to appear.
(Let there be one boy, one girl; no, two girls to fill it out.)
And the children must be outfitted in varied rhythms
swelling to crescendo as they enter
to compare with tremulous songbirds high up on the tree;
and the birds must be contrasted, gifted with proper names,
branches to highlight and counterpoint their luscious tones.
And then an image must be drawn out of the tree itself
while I count on the wind to bring everything around,
the night falling so a listener will know I made this up,
and take not too lightly how it resolves,
missing thereby the still essential harmony and dissonance
which was His answer when I began to speak.

"Let Me Tell You about Happiness"

Quick, let me have it, I need the word.
But mine, not yours you soaked in honeysuckle,
then delivered to the front door this morning
where, unsuspecting, I answered in pajamas
to catch you unaware: shining, baby-blue gabardine suit,
blue tie, a little blue book in your hands,
the shiny gold letters promising secrets within
for those who admitted you. I didn't, of course.
But after I slammed the door I squinted
through the curtains to take in the '65 Ford,
its back seat a swarm of kids swaddled in blue
you would have let loose on my own and on my wife
had I given an inch. And her beside you,
a blue snood streaming with fuchsia ribbons,
shot me her index finger three times
(I thought of Him three times raising the Cross
before He ascended) and stuck her tongue out thrice.
And so began another Sunday in our funny kingdom.

Rhapsody

This light reflecting light within a child's face
approximates what they once called the holy.
Here at my son's nursery school, squatting a chair
beside him, a half-dozen lit like him
encircling our table, I am a celebrant.
Blue-smocked little priests, the boys and girls
hunch over their work to which my son invited me:
it is only the world they reshape out of their clay,
the cosmos as three characters they smash, remake again:
a man, a woman, and a snake this rolling pin
is handed me to imitate. All afternoon I do what I am told.
Meanwhile the radiance thickens toward rain
in the city outside, assuming I'll return
the same man. I will. But smaller, I hope,
each instant knocking on the next one to let me in.

The Joshua Tree

Squatting mornings beside his crib,
awash in first light while sleep tosses him,
I have sailed for centuries in my son's face:
back to the origin of the tree
outside our window, its dagger-shaped, its spine-tipped
named for his namesake when he arose,
a warrior against his enemies,
on some plain which had divided from a marsh
eons before in the primeval.
Back to the origin of the sun
which even as the day proceeds will slip
between the lineaments of clouds only to come again.
By such squints and hintings you reveal yourself,
Invisible, giving me this child as you gave yourself
just one and spoke through Him a little while.
Listen. In this hush I am whispering to mine.
Shh. Shh. Shh. Shh. Shh. I tell myself.
When he wakes up he will begin to leave you.

In Advent

Tonight I will suffer one star
to process above the others.
Suffer the flocks to cease
their bleating, lift one stare
skyward for the march.
Suffer the dung, the straw, the lowing,
the wise, the vessel of the mother,
the child, all one assembled at the crèche.
And then, no part of them, this young man
dumbfounded, kneeling in radiance.
Joseph, it is you I turn to
my twenty-three years a father.
You who have husbanded firmaments
yet come away convinced.
What trembling brought you to your knees
to take some other father's son
onto yourself, suspending everything?
At the edge of this page I bless your piety.
Suffer the myth to continue you
after I and my kind are gone.

The Looms of Our Mothers

Robert Cooper

The strands I find tangle in my fingers
Their names first are lost from me then their lives
Whose parents these children are still linger
Though the ways scars do wormlike from knives
Long ago oiled and sheathed in memory.

Memory   Saint Augustine has taught us
Is visceral   the mind's own craw its belly
Or it is he said sometimes where we regress
And strangle in their bed the sequelae
Of our lost past   Memory is the womb
Also   It is what makes us all mothers
Who bend over those strands that thread the loom
Of our mind through all its wide or narrow rooms
We pick what dear fine dust we can recover

All Souls' Morning

County Kerry, Ireland

Robert Cording

Jittery light, scraps of wind, the monotone of rain.
Is it the thrushes moving across the poor cloth
Of grass that brings my grandmother to the margin
Of memory? I'd come from classes twice a month

To eat with her. All those women, moving in unison,
Fitting and stitching. Clattering machines. "Piece-work,"
My grandmother called it. She's back at work again,
Tethered this time to her husband's death. In the dark

She rises to cook breakfast for two. Later she dusts
His pictures, habits of grief shaping her round of days.
She tends the dead the way these cows in their pendulous
Plodding way cross from unlit barn to field, that haze

Of expectation always in their wet eyes. They stand
And feed, nuzzle the short, depleted grass into milk.
Mornings I bring my small faith to the close at hand;
Just now the blued iridescent wing of a common rook

Offers itself to my eye. Sparks of flinty sun.
Gone in rain's let-downs. Glimmerings and blurs.
On time, the co-op tractor stops in the stubborn rain,
Here to collect the morning's milk. A widow, two doors

Down, will invite the driver in for tea. "They'll marry,"
My neighbor's said, his eyes kindling with the thought

Of their rising again from hurts. And him, he's "lucky
To have a good job": he waves hello now through the mist

And I see again how his face, reddish-yellow, is raw
From the chemicals he handles. After his lungs gave
Way to asbestos-crazed cells bred thirty years before
In the rat-grey dark of a second job he had to have,

My grandfather said, "Hell, the pay was good and when
I came up from the dark, the cars and dirty roads
Were never brighter, never as clear." Wind and rain,
Smoke and mist, spots of sun interceding like words

That rise up at oddest moments to make the world
Always there suddenly apparent. Quick as breath,
The hours go by, a rook sweeps sideways on wind,
Threads a needle's hole of light as if on faith.

The world keeps moving to its tasks, random with pain,
Rich with surprise. The tractor's gone off with the milk,
The cows turn to shoots of grass raised by the rain,
I write: *In backlit mist, the thrushes' feathers are silk.*

Prayer

October, the air filmed as if with tears, and time
Stalled between the light-hearted leaf fall of ashes

And the clenched hearts of oak leaves
That stay put like misery.

There is a sadness my mother cannot escape.

Twice a week she greets her mother's silent stone
With flowers, with pictures,

Once with an unsent letter. She goes on reaching

For the phone she tells me. Twice a day
For fifty years it carried their quarrel of damaged love.

Her mother's death was graceless.
A waiting for pills, for her lungs to fill again,

For the suffocating
Pain of breath and the fear of its departure.

For some sign of love denied.

What did you think of her face? my mother wants to know.
Daily, the scowl death froze on her mother's forehead,

Her distended mouth, waits to be recalled.

Each skirmish, even the littlest
Stray remark buried under years heavier than stones

Is held up now for long scrutiny.

Each room of this house holds their rankling talk,
The two of them sworn to opposing ways.

And all that while their hopes were twinned
As in those letters of North and South,

Each opposing soldier a river apart, each homesick,
Dreaming of "taking a loved one by the hand before long."

My mother leans against the window
As if it were a palm against her cheek. Outside,

The lines of vision are longer,

Avenues between the unleafed ashes. The undersides
Of clouds bloom pinks and reds

And the sun expands at the horizon
As it must have for John Keats after he'd imagined

The world's misery as a school for his soul.

After the Civil War, survivors from both sides gathered
Once a year.

Together they watched the ravaged fields turn to grass.

Perhaps they knew the charity
Of a world large enough to contain their sorrow.

Perhaps peace fills in whatever space can be cleared for it.

Perhaps stone by stone rolled away, we raise our dead.

Assisi

Even in February the buses came and climbed the hill,
The Umbrian light an angel's wing in cloud,

Glowing from some unknowable source in an Italian painting.
No wonder some gave a life's savings to see Saint Francis's

City of pink stone. No wonder we couldn't help loving
Those arching crypts, blue and storied as a child's heaven.

What we want to remember, we do. How he could keep on giving
His one robe, unashamed by love. How his love never failed

The sick, the poor, the criminal. Even a war in Arezzo
Simply disappeared, like rain into sunlight, Saint Francis

Undoing the daily harm no one could ever alter in his life.
The demons said to be in all of us laid down their weapons,

Taken by such tenderness. Everyone was forgiven in Giotto's picture.
Saint Francis went on, unable to sleep, so many blessings

Still needed to be given. He walked all the way to Mt. La Verna.
When we close our eyes, we can see him hold out his hands.

The wounds bleed into them and into his body, the marks
Of another life. From then on, he grew thinner until he was

Gone, his love absolute. At least once, someone saw him
Come back, robed in light. Giotto would have us believe

It was only a dream of what we cannot stop imagining.
We came back all winter, listening to the monks tell his story

Until word for word, we could repeat it.

Clonmacnois: A Short History

It's deserted except for the light
Gliding over exhausted stone, the rain
That wakes a steam of ghosts above

The grass. Rooks grip the wind's edge,
Wishbones of lightning break against
The black wings of trees, and the sky

Floods with sun and storm. There are
Two towers, eight ruined churches,
Three crosses, a vast field of graves

Like volumes of history too numerous
For anyone to make sense of.
Centuries ago this city was a vision,

Saint Ciaran opening his eyes on
A huge flowering tree, its fruitful
Branches a place for birds to come and eat.

A monastery grew up, drew boatloads
Of students who wanted to climb
Ladders of wisdom, to learn the love

Of saints. There were raids, fires,
Plunderings—a thousand years of violence,
A thousand years of prayers for love

To match it. Saint Ciaran appeared
For centuries, looming up at marauders,
Carrying his crozier as if to heal them:

A story which took years to imagine,
Which was needed to balance the raids
That kept coming. This city was lost

And saved and lost again, preserved now
In ruin. Only the stories continue:
Some see horrible scenes of slaughter

In the night sky above Clonmacnois;
Others see boats, yearning upwards,
Sails filled with star-pearled air.

April 7

Allowing her to see my fears, I asked her what sort of death I would die. She answered with a very tender smile: "God will sip you up like a little drop of dew."

David Craig

And she was right.
Mother Agnes, 54 revolutions later:
first the coma, was sipped, as if the taste
demanded pause: the long, quiet life,
like each of ours, each soul
gathered to a final draw.
She loved as one always must,
in silence.

Dorothy Day called it the long loneliness,
the wine glass lifted: small puddles,
the wet shake of birds beneath wind
and a shifting rain from trees.
Tall grass, running along the convent
wall. The speed of gray clouds, how they
become our lives, all the beauty here;
we feel what we cannot hold, only contain.
It's the God we cannot have:
leaving, staying. How does the grass stand
the pain? How do we?

What courage it takes to live here,
anything given in a world
running like clouds.

May 21–26

"The Holy Innocents will not be little children in heaven; they will have only the indefin-
able charms of childhood. They are represented as 'children' because we need pictures to un-
derstand spiritual things. . . . Yes, I hope to join them! If they want, I'll be their little page,
holding up their trains."

The muffled silence. A procession,
all the townspeople, gone under the hill.
They will be great on our flanks, bobbing
like trolls: the big hats, the almost-voices.

Their singing will be their own,
and we will be with them.

What will we be able to make of it,
those voices: the ones that were
ours as we called beneath ourselves,
muttering, Popeyes, in a kind of glossolalia,
over the hard paths of our lives?

We saw the tree split in the forest.
The fumes singed our nostril hair.
We saw all the wet grass, mornings,
but we were someplace else, listening
to other voices. We were those voices,
too, and we knew. It was clear
as the rings in our noses, as clear
as the distance and cover provided.

We got in line.
Started singing, rough axes

over our shoulders.
The trees belonged to us there.
We had many short friends and were happy.

June 4

"Don't be astonished if I don't appear to you after my death, and if you see nothing extraordinary as a sign of my happiness. You will remember that it's 'my little way' not to desire to see anything."

God, who with all His might,
lifts the grass from the dew,
rumbles the earth around
on its stone axis,
strains to create peas.
See His hammock swing,
hear His reaction, cool burst
of lemonade. It gives Him joy
to put His ear to His chest,
to hear the old clock working.
Up again, He pulls down the red
shade of night, lingers, two eyes
just above the sea. Big ships,
freighters, cruise past,
each little life on board,
each sniffle: His province,
the garden of His concern.

Come down now. Where birds might
settle on your hand, where a woman
named Linda might come into your life.
A place where the only payment
you can give is silence, like movement
in a world, right as a man
jacking up his car. The road sounds:
vehicles passing, dust flying up.
Maybe some old guy watching you,
gurning on tobacco.

Talk if you want to,
or don't.

There is this world. You are of it:
big sun, Texaco stations, rows
of candy. Some guy in uniform
who wants to sell you air.

June 4

A little later, being alone with her, and seeing her suffer very much, I said: "Well, you wanted to suffer, and God hasn't forgotten it."

Death, our little pal with the big teeth,
like the piranha my friend has mounted
in his kitchen: each tooth, an incisor,
each fishy happy enough to hang
like a Japanese lantern from your hide,
leaving you bone and the river.
And the river won't mind, one more
undulation to move, the joy in the noise
it will find itself making. Your bones,
half-submerged, will shine, white
in the sun. You will be like the man
in the white hat, and the sun will ache
to have such playmates. White on white,
the two of you will wash the scene
in light. Maybe a native will canoe by,
see you there. He will look for a moment,
move on. You will have had your spree.
But more time will come and take you;
you will collapse in a heap,
meet more of the river.

Who could give this? The arch of back,
the voice she kept inside her, silent,
like a field of headless chickens, their
inarticulate bobbings. How slowly
they lie down, the only noise the sound
their feet make, stepping dumbly
over each other. The occasional flap
of wing. All of this would be absurd

if you were not of it, if you did not arch
a little bit in their going.

This is what she gave, the untuning.
You are there, too, if you read this.
Welcome to the provinces, where you are
the sleek curve and spitting sound through
water whales make, their shiny eel-like move
as they submerge. This is us again:
into sunlight, back to grief. One, our home,
the other, our story. We fish here,
Mr. and Mrs. Janus, a group called the Optics.
Grab a net, feel the rock in the boat.

In My Father's House

Linda Craig

Like a mime palming walls
which keep only the white face prisoner
which only the white gloves can fathom,
I reach for You.

These walls are mirrors
lost to dirt
fingered "REMEMBER MAN
THAT THOU ART DUST AND UNTO DUST
THOU SHALT RETURN."

Jesus said, "In my Father's house
are many mansions."
The mime slides a trampoline on stage;
the tall black hat settles firmly on the head
with each new ascent,
is left up there
with each new fall.

The Housewife's Paradise

Peter Davison

Across the scene dance dromedaries,
tigers, prancing horses, zebras,
"two and two of all flesh
wherein is the breath of life."
The sceptre tail of Lion commands
a procession of beasts under father trees.
The sky has clouded over. Waters gurgle
to tug the ark by its hull. Will Noah preserve
one pair of every sort of genital,
the periphrastic families of the earth?

In Pennsylvania preacher Edward Hicks,
fleeing from ghostly swords,
peered through the branches of a half-cut forest
and brushed in scenes of peaceful time-to-come
as promised in plain statements by the Lord.
A hatted Quaker smacked a friendly palm
against a feathered red man's on a beach.
Smiling Lion crouched to nibble hay
by the side of pussycat Ox.
Leaves did not tumble, wounds did not leak blood,
lambkins never crumpled in a colic.
Rooftops, safe against God's lightning,
kept rainspots off the pewter plates of housewives,
sheltering the honeyed entropies of peace.

On working farms the gravid ewes give
bloody birth on bare barn floors. The lambs
lie there, at first unblinking. Mothers lick

mucus from the nostrils and the eyes,
and offspring totter to suck at the flesh
that further heats their breath.
In May longlight, February lambs
may drop the teat and munch the sea of grass
as noisily as their great toothed sisters,
and then, why not, next fall, be mounted
by the greedy-shouldered ram
with gasps of satisfaction, breath of life?

In Hicks' landscapes horses won't gallop:
they prance, curvet, lie at rest.
Even George Washington's steed stands easy,
deaf to captains and the shouting.
The Peaceable Kingdom, shelter for Friends,
shelters them coolly under a cloudless roof
in a clearing as solid as a square stone house.

Here is the land of cider, laundry, bread,
the housewife's paradise, with love lavishly spread
in quilt or bright-scrubbed doorstep
to shed its inner light
and banish every howling of the spirit.
Cast it out elsewhere, anywhere you will,
and pit the blessed order of a kitchen shelf
against the barbarism of the kill.

Paradise As a Garden

For Elizabeth B. Moynihan

One of the great tautologies: self-regarding:
in which the seeds of growth
are the kernels of contemplation,
in which the contemplation of desire
ekes out desire's last sigh,
in which what enlarges the space
is its surrounding hedges:
husk and flower are one.

These were no northern sprawls, however,
no meadows of bluets and flax.
In Persia water collected itself, at whatever
cost, within walls: model of a house or city:
no water, no life. Yet sometimes paradise
persisted as boundaries only, and in the end
the garden stood, bracelets of stone and water,
without leaf, flower, or fruit to carry temptation.

And so it follows, through ages, crosses and tongues,
that when we speak of our eternal delight,
whether a garden we were once expelled from
or one that has been lost and overgrown,
it is the edges we cannot forget.
Whatever persists within, forever fresh,
is the indelible border of imagination.

The Fall of the Dolls' House

The family figurines sat round a fire
at the hearth of a dolls' house, porcelain-faced,
dove-breasted, leaning against each other,
smiling as though their rage were ruled by music,
the transcendental chords of Plato's dream.
Father, a kindly provider, judge, and priest,
Mother, a milkmaid, mending things, healing,
Children at play, at rest, reading their lessons—
such are the lessons that our lessons taught.
A window-frame hemmed in this perfect scene
for all to worship, as we worship icons.

Beside the dolls' house that the family built
the father's drunk. His wife weeps for her sex.
Young Tim is crippled and will surely die.
The older children dream of rape and murder,
for which of them has strength enough to act
as ancestor? The dolls' house shows them how
all parents fail, the Virgin fails the Child.
Their icon topples before war, change, chaos;
embraces yield to riots in the streets.
The pulse beats hard when Manson or Attila
kicks in the fire door, wrestles down Papá,
mugs mother, rapes the girl, snaps like twigs
the GI crutches of poor Tiny Tim.

Look at the dolls' house my grandparents owned
(its furniture imported from Saxe-Coburg)
in this contented photo. In another
the harmony of Diderot and Newton
takes on the dissonance of Marx and Freud.
My parents' glamor hints a naughty streak:

their dolls wear knickers, camisoles, bandeaux.
In a more recent snap, my wife and I,
nurtured on Tillich, Kierkegaard, Jung,
wear casual clothes but strike a mannered pose.
I slouch eccentric, while she smiles, protecting
the children underneath a cherry tree.
We'll leave the house, I think. The leaves are falling.

My children see themselves as in a poster:
unisex, well-provided, amplified.
Shatter the house, my darlings, helter-skelter!
The harmonies of our philosophy
have let us sleep through years of cuckoo-clocks
in drawing-rooms of matchsticks, cards, and lace.
If you are granted wishes for the world,
enlarge its scope: make work as one with play
in houses built for everlasting fire
where man and woman burn like seraphim.

La Cathédrale Engloutie

An ancient place. The roofs are high and grey.
A friend and I walk down a cobbled street.
I've never seen an alleyway so neat:
brisk brooms have swept each speck of dust away.

No motor, tire or wheel makes hiss or clatter
across the squares of past the whitewashed angles.
My friend says, "poor and rich agree: no wrangles!
Here nothing has ever seemed to be the matter."

In the cathedral square the Church stands fast:
its leaded panes of red and blue depict
a squad of sturdy saints, with spires erect
unsmirched by soot or by iconoclast.

Within, black hats and furled umbrellas press
past chapels of mahogany, toward cages
that stand behind the apse, to bank their wages
and scribble checks where sinners once confessed.

Observe the great south aisle, the Bishop's Tomb:
walk out into the nave. No monk or priest
makes antiphon, and no one kneels. From east
to west a flock of tables fills the room,

and banqueters participate in revel.
They dance and drink from foamy steins of beer
between the speeches. How they love to hear
that cash has saved the country from the devil!

"Listen, my friend, what made your family chafe
to live in any other town? Why here?"
We walk in silence through another square.
"The schools are good," he sighs. "The streets are safe."

Penance

Stuart Dybek

It was always Good Friday
those Saturday afternoons.
Stooped babkas in black coats
and babushkas, kneeling
in marble aisles
before racks of vigil candles,
faces buried in hands.
Weeping echoed through the dim church
as foreign as their droned
language of prayer.
I stood in line
waiting the priest's question,
"Alone or with others?"
and my turn in Confession,
trying to imagine
the terrible sins of old women.

Confession

FATHER BOGUSLAW was the priest
I waited for,
the one whose breath,
through the thin partition
of the confessional,
reminded me of the ventilator
behind Vic's Tap.

He huffed and smacked
as if in response to my dull litany
of sins, and I pictured him
slouched in his cubicle,
draped in vestments,
the way he sat slumped
in the back entrance to the sacristy
before saying morning mass—
hungover, sucking an unlit Pall Mall,
exhaling smoke.

Once, his head thudded
against the wooden box.
Father, I whispered, Father,
but he was out, snoring.
I knelt, wondering what to do,
until he finally groaned
and hacked himself awake.

As always, I'd saved the deadly sins for last:
the lies and copied homework,
snitched drinks, ditching school,

hitch-hiking, which I'd been convinced
was an offense against the Fifth Commandment
which prohibited suicide.

Before I reached the dirty snapshots
of Korean girls, stolen from the dresser
of my war hero Uncle Al,
and still unrepentantly cached
behind the oil shed,
he knocked
and said I was forgiven.

As for Penance:
Go in peace, my son,
I'm suffering enough today
for both of us.

Benediction

At dusk, I traced the peddler's hymn
to the misted mouth
of a viaduct that swallowed full moons
and red comets of streaking tail-lights.
Perhaps, on the other side,
a horizon stretched.
Then, overhead, a border of boxcars
thundered by
and I turned back to aisles of neon.

Night was narrow—
a strip of darkness between shopsigns.
Snow fell from the height
of a streetlamp.
I knew the names of seven
attending angels
but was seventeen before I saw
my first jay.

Yet, I worshiped the natural world
as only an immigrant can
love his adopted country—
the one he should have been born in.
For me, the complexity of a grasshopper
catapulting from the Congo
behind a billboard
was an irrefutable proof
for the God of a baffling order.

And in my heart, I still kneel
on a boulevard in summer
seeking benediction
beneath the glittering cross
of a dragonfly.

Icon

Our Lady of Sorrows,
the Black Virgin of Czestochowa,
became my girl friend. Once,
while praying, I saw her smile.
And every morning was a requiem
or the Feast Day of a martyr—
the priest in black or red,
cortege of traffic, headlights
funneling through incense
under viaducts. While my surplice
settled around me like smoke,
my father rode the blue spark
of a streetcar to the foundry
where, in the dark mornings,
the blackened windows glowed
like stained glass.

Saint Clare

She refused to marry when she was twelve and was so impressed by a Lenten sermon of
Saint Francis in 1212 that she ran away from her home in Assisi, received her habit, and
took the vow of absolute poverty. Since Francis did not yet have a convent for women, he
placed her in the Benedictine convent near Basia, where she was joined by her younger
sister, Agnes. Her father sent twelve armed men to bring Agnes back, but Clare's prayers
rendered her so heavy they were unable to budge her.
—*John H. Delaney*, Pocket Dictionary of Saints

Louise Erdrich

1   The Call

First I heard the voice throbbing across the river.
I saw the white phosphorescence of his robe.
As he stepped from the boat, as he walked
there spread from each footfall a black ripple,
from each widening ring a wave,
from the waves a sea that covered the moon.
So I was seized in total night
and I abandoned myself in his garment
like a fish in a net. The slip knots
tightened on me and I rolled
until the sudden cry hauled me out.
Then this new element, a furnace of mirrors,
in which I watch myself burn.
The scales of my old body melt away like coins,
for I was rich, once, and my father
had already chosen my husband.

2   Before

I kept my silver rings in a box of porphyrite.
I ate salt on bread. I could sew.
I could mend the petals of a rose.
My nipples were pink, my sister's brown.
In the fall we filled our wide skirts with walnuts
for our mother to crack with a wooden hammer.
She put the whorled meats into our mouths,
closed our lips with her finger
and said to Hush. So we slept
and woke to find our bodies arching into bloom.
It happened to me first,
the stain on the linen, the ceremonial
seal which was Eve's fault.
In the church at Assisi I prayed. I listened
to Brother Francis and I took his vow.
The embroidered decorations at my bodice
turned real, turned to butterflies and were dispersed.
The girdle of green silk, the gift from my father
slithered from me like a vine,
so I was something else that grew from air,
and I was light, the skeins of hair
that my mother had divided with a comb of ivory
were cut from my head and parceled to the nesting birds.

3   My Life As a Saint

I still have the nest, now empty,
woven of my hair, of the hollow grass,
and silken tassels at the ends of seeds.
From the window where I prayed,
I saw the house wrens gather

dark filaments from air
in the shuttles of their beaks.
Then the cup was made fast
to the body of the tree,
bound with the silver excresence of the spider,
and the eggs, four in number,
ale gold and trembling,
curved in a thimble of down.

The hinged beak sprang open, tongue erect,
screaming to be fed
before the rest of the hatchling emerged.
I did not eat. I smashed my bread to crumbs upon the sill
for the parents were weary as God is weary.
We have the least mercy on the one
who created us,
who introduced us to this hunger.

The smallest mouth starved and the mother
swept it out like rubbish with her wing.
I found it that dawn, after lauds,
already melting into the heat of the flagstone,
a transparent teaspoon of flesh,
the tiny beak shut, the eyes still sealed
within a membrane of the clearest blue.

I buried the chick in a box of leaves
The rest grew fat and clamorous.
I put my hand through the thorns one night and felt the bowl,
the small brown begging bowl,
waiting to be filled.

By morning, the strands of the nest disappear
into each other, shaping
an emptiness within me that I make lovely

as the immature birds make the air
by defining the tunnels and the spirals
of the new sustenance. And then,
no longer hindered by the violence of their need,
they take to other trees, fling themselves
deep into the world.

4   *Agnes*

When you entered the church at Basia
holding the sceptor of the almond's
white branch, and when you struck
the bedrock floor, how was I to know
the prayer would be answered?
I heard the drum of hooves long in the distance,
and I held my forehead to the stone of the altar.
I asked for nothing. It is almost
impossible to ask for nothing.
I have spent my whole life trying.

I know you felt it, when his love spilled.
That ponderous light. From then on you endured
happiness, the barge you pulled
as I pull mine. This
is called density of purpose.
As you learned, you must shed everything else
in order to bear it.

That is why, toward the end of your life,
when at last there was nothing I could not relinquish,
I allowed you to spring forward without me.
Sister, I unchained myself. For I was always
the heaviest passenger,

the stone wagon of example,
the freight you dragged all the way to heaven,
and how were you to release yourself
from me, then, poor mad horse,
except by reaching the gate?

Villa de Matel
Houston

Sybil Estess

At twilight an old nun paddles toward me
in her life-jacket, bright blue. I am so
quiet for the day at the retreat house.

Here, women believe things are possible,
even the impossible. . . . They start with
exercise on summer evenings before

any dim night of the soul. The lady
says she is glad I have come for the day
to pray—although I'm Protestant. She says

she assumes never again will there be
a convent as big as this one. For God,
she claims, is a spirit of change. Acres

here in the city are gardened, Eden-
like. Geraniums, hibiscus, fountains,
grottos, paths wind everywhere to statues

of the Virgin. The nun says she thanks Christ
all the time for Vatican II, floating folks
like her and me together. She works with

cancer patients, sees that the Lord never
notices what denomination any suffering
woman is, or dying man. . . .

She hastens to say that parents should not
wait for the church, but teach God themselves
to their own. She whispers this between breaths,

while stroking. It is good, I say, she does
not swim alone. At her age, a body-
buoy—blue as Mary's mantilla—brings

brilliant company. Near fifty, I try
laps when my aged confidante leaves me
in indigo silence. I will to believe.

all things visible and invisible:
clear, blue pool; green crickets, chirping high up
in palms; black evening; change; children; her peace.

On Jesus, Taking His Word on Immortality

Robert A. Fink

Not a question of belief.
The Bible says even devils believe
and tremble, their humped backs smoldering
still, horns curled black
recalling the jagged heat of light,
the length of a scream falling.
It is, instead, a matter of faith:
saying to the mountains, *Move!*,
telling a cripple *rise up and walk*,
or doing what we do as if
each story were being written down
somewhere in red letters. It is patience:
learning to watch for the sea
to sift mountains down to size
thin enough for pockets
or skimming flat across the water.
It is waiting for the man to give it up—
the old alms game, eyes hard behind dark glasses,
one leg folded back until the night
and home down alleys narrow as the eye of storms.
Can we count the hairs of a head?
Or clothe ourselves in lilies?
It is harder than belief.
It is what we pray to find at the end of poems.

My Sons Ask Where God Lives

When I was eight I asked Miss Reese,
long as her dresses, hair
thin as snakes dangling to her belt.
She read the Bible every hour just in case.
There was nothing she had missed.
Miss Reese kept me nights
my folks were out of town,
sent me off to sleep with prophets
calling flames from heaven, the earth opening
to swallow wicked kids, a pit of fire for unbelievers.
She made it easy to believe.

At Sunday School, the picture on the wall was kind,
pretty as Freddy Johnson's mother.
Children tumbled everywhere,
all colors. Jesus hugged them like his own.
Every Sunday I looked for me
and the pit that must be in a lower corner
disguised—a well, water the color of sulfur.
I wanted to believe Miss Reese was wrong,
Jesus never frowned, but I remembered
he cleared the temple with a whip
and only picked one thief for heaven.

I realize this is no answer.
The pretty God lived on the wall in Sunday School.
I tried to find him in my heart
where they said he was. All but Miss Reese
who knew he hid in alleys waiting for a boy
slipped out from church to ride his Schwinn
or try Dad's pipe.
Her God smiled straight as the shiv

he'd slip between the first and second ribs
and twist until he hollowed out a pit,
fit habitation in the gut,
a dripping wound that never healed.

Foot Reflexologist, Farmers and Christmas

For twenty bucks an hour, the old and lame
remove their shoes and line up
at the LA-Z-BOY recliner
to wait their turn at Sister Thelma's fingers
realigning withered feet.
Their looks confess no doubts
about this mobile home, double-wide,
parked among the scrub oak
just beyond the city limits.
They know the cost of specialists:
the crisp receptionist,
the chromium waiting room
reflecting everything but pain.
So they gladly queue up at the trailer
in Big Mac overalls and gingham dresses
to swap testimonials and sip the herbal tea
Sister Thelma's agile daughter serves
with last year's bumper crop of sweet potatoes.

Their children,
who took degrees in agriculture,
shake their heads at old folk
sowing cold hard cash to every prevailing wind
that skims the topsoil from farmed-out land.
They put *their* faith in two-story tractors
and meteorologists dependable as the six o'clock news.
They've learned better than to argue with parents
who profess the enigma of a family farm,
still holding to the garden
and a few chickens.

Yet every Christmas, the kids and grandkids gather
at the kitchen table smoothed by elbows
of three generations, to feast again
on stories only the oldest and the youngest can believe:
How on December 24, 1943, an angel
stepped into a foxhole outside Taranto, Italy,
where a farm boy fresh from the States
prayed softly, bleeding, counting stars
through broken limbs of winter trees.
And the angel laid his hands upon the wound
and prophesied good news:
Peace. A slight limp.
A hundred-acre farm in Oklahoma.

The Bog Sacrifice

John Finlay

The iron and acid water of the bog,
Rising and falling with the winter rains,
Two thousand years, preserved him as he died,
Pinned naked to the floor by wooden crooks.
No fire had cut and cleaned the clotted soul.
Runic stakes, washed white as salt, were laid
Over his narrow breast, sunk in the peat.

The sacrificial rope they hanged him from,
Of woven skins, still cut into his throat,
Tight as when death came. His gentle face,
Forced upward by the torsion of the noose,
Bore with monstrous discipline his bane,
As loose ends, like serpents, meandered down
His naked length, pressed into his flesh.

A cap of wolfskin hived his shaven head.
Descended from a line of conscript priests,
He died in youth, still delicate and whole.
When he was lifted from the pit, the earth
Itself then sweating like an ancient beast,
He looked as if alive. Faint cries of snipes
Brought sunlight piercing to his closing eyes.

Before Christ reached this isolated north,
A chthonic goddess, holding iron breasts,
Each year in early spring exacted death.
In winter when the winds blew keen off ice,

Or summer with its rippling swarm of weeds,
The bog seemed never raised above the sea,
But underneath, out of whose depths she came.

Job, Too

Nola Garrett

What if your best is mediocrity—
say second violin in the Erie Philharmonic
wearing black and bowing (always
blending)? Your undistinguished cells
begin lens hardening exactly at forty;
no optometrist is surprised
how valiantly you've contended
with the always blending print.
And what of these other scars: on
the left knee; the episiotomy; the divorce
decree? All common, not extraordinary—
no reason to call the cops, the EPA.

These things happen, too: the woman
with one sunken eye who still can't watch
murder movies, the Nazi technician
who lived in Cleveland so long the smokestacks
ceased to remind him of anything.
It's only in games—the snap of someone else's aces,
your esteemed opponent's brilliant cross,
the baseball's sweet thwack and arc
up up up, lost, but falling clearly
beyond the foul line—that the thin red-bound
rules are observed, the umpire always there.

Job, too, was a game. The story of a game,
told with Job a sort of willing chess man
parked awhile near the ashes

and then seemingly restored to play,
to age, to remember what might have been:
those three lively daughters whose brothers
"would send and invite to eat and drink."
The slender rules, unknown to Job,
protected only him. We read the story
again and again because after the pain
and the hard arguing over blame,
comes a slippery moment of clarity,
a creative suspension of the rules.

Our slippery best, these days, may be
Shit happens, a bumper sticker
above the whirling exhaust which suggests
no source: no divine sphincter.
Consider, though, the pleasure of exploring
upstream where the lush grass grows near
the narrowing banks, and, midcreek,
Clinton Hale's holsteins alternate
drinking with gazing into their milky pasts.
Occasionally, one humps up like a Cadillac
and pees her twisting gold. Then another,
as if it were an original thought, humps
too, and plops what's left after gold
and milk have been strained from dandelions,
perennial rye, and yesterday's dew.

Guide to the Other Gallery

Dana Gioia

This is the hall of broken limbs
Where splintered marble athletes lie
Beside the arms of cherubim.
Nothing is ever thrown away.

These butterflies are set in rows.
So small and gray inside their case
They look alike now. I suppose
Death makes most creatures commonplace.

These portraits here of the unknown
Are hung three high, frame piled on frame.
Each potent soul who craved renown,
Immortalized without a name.

Here are the shelves of unread books,
Millions of pages turning brown.
Visitors wander through the stacks,
But no one ever takes one down.

I wish I were a better guide.
There's so much more that you should see.
Rows of bottles with nothing inside.
Displays of locks which have no key.

You'd like to go? I wish you could.
This room has such a peaceful view.
Look at that case of antique wood
Without a label. It's for you.

All Souls'

Suppose there is no heaven and no hell,
And that the dead can never leave the earth,
That, as the body rots, the soul breaks free,
Weak and disabled in its second birth.

And then invisible, rising to the light,
Each finds a world it cannot touch or hear,
Where colors fade and, if the soul cries out,
The silence stays unbroken in the air.

How flat the ocean seems without its roar,
Without the sting of salt, the bracing gust.
The sunset blurs into a grayish haze.
The morning snowfall is a cloud of dust.

The pines that they revisit have no scent.
They cannot feel the needled forest floor.
Crossing the stream, they watch the current flow
Unbroken as they step down from the shore.

They want their voices to become the wind—
Intangible like them— to match its cry,
Howling in treetops, covering the moon,
Tumbling the storm clouds in a rain-swept sky.

But they are silent as a rising mist,
A smudge of smoke dissolving in the air.
They watch the shadows lengthen on the grass.
The pallor of the rose is their despair.

The Burning Ladder

                    Jacob
never climbed the ladder
burning in his dream. Sleep
pressed him like a stone
in the dust,
                    and when
he should have risen
like a flame to join
that choir, he was sick
of travelling,
                    and closed
his eyes to the Seraphim
ascending, unconscious
of the impossible distances
between their steps,
                    missed
them mount the brilliant
ladder, slowly disappearing
into the scattered light
between the stars,
                    slept
through it all, a stone
upon a stone pillow,
shivering. Gravity
always greater than desire.

Instructions for the Afternoon

I.

Leave the museums, the comfortable rooms,
the safe distractions of the masterpiece.
The broken goddesses have lost their voice,
the martyr's folded hands no longer bless.
Footsteps echo through the palaces
where no one lives. Consider what you've come for.

Leave the museums. Find the dark churches
in back towns that history has forgotten,
the unimportant places the powerful ignore
where commerce knows no profit will be made.
Sad hamlets at the end of silted waterways,
dry mountain villages where time
is the thin shadow of an ancient tower
that moves across the sundazed pavement of the square
and disappears each evening without trace.

Make the slow climb up the winding alleys.
Walk between houses shuttered close for midday
and overhear the sound of other lives,
the conversations in the language you
will never learn. Make the long ascent
up to the grey stone chapel on the hillside
when summer is a furnace open to the world,
and pause there breathless in the blinding sun
only one moment, then enter.

                        For this
is how it must be seen to understand:
by walking from the sunlight into darkness,

117

by groping down the aisle
as your wet skin cools and your eyes adjust,
by finding what you've come for thoughtlessly,
shoved off into a corner, almost lost
among the spectacle of gold and purple.

Here in the half-light, covered by the years
it will exist. And wait,
wait like a mirror in an empty room
whose resolutions are invisible
to anyone but you. Wait like the stone
face of a statue waits, forever frozen
or poised in the moment before action.

II.

But if the vision fails, and the damp air
stinks of summer must and disrepair,
if the worn steps rising to the altar
lead nowhere but to stone, this, too, could be
the revelation—but of a destiny
fixed as the graceless frescoes on the wall—
the grim and superannuated gods
who rule this shadow-land of marble tombs,
bathed in its green suboceanic light.
Not a vision to pursue, and yet
these insufficiencies make up the world.
Strange how all journeys come to this: the sun
bright on the unfamiliar hills, new vistas
dazzling the eye, the stubborn heart unchanged.

Light Beneath the Skin (or Pronoun 2)

Diane Glancy

I am holy yours, sweet Christ.
Savior on the road
when I come transfixed.
The blackjam just let out of the jar.
Still a hook in the treetop my love.
Sweet Christ.
I've found nothing else.
Your covering of blood for my heart.
I pack my suitcase
and the garden with asparagus spears in it. The spiked stalks taller each
time I look. I pack the black and white linoleum, and all the blood gravy
fallen into the cracks. I pack the chicken hearts red and dark as rosebuds.
I'm coming, Lord Christ. To be then yours under a lock of trees.
Emollients of rain. A sound not yet made by a single lark flying in a treed
field. Broken now has to be whole in Christ. I float up the long hallways
of rain. Over the waiting shingles, the hard boards of my heart.

Theology of Deer

The jazz-bows of earth
their roll through space
traveling farther each day
the cherubim on drum
a trumpet of angels
the beats of an old life
a smaller inverted mind
when you get saved
the night you stop on the road through the Cattaraugus Reservation to
watch the northern lights. The crowd of spirits. Their migration to the rez.
Tuning Indian cars. Holding babies in their arms. When a deer crosses the
road in the fog behind you. You think Christ for a moment it is him. And
you say *dude of dudes and deer of deers.*

The Transformation Band

Behind an old car on the road
yez I could have washed out
like the Creek County bridge
but Christ redeemers me
hyster huckstar Christ
the *phlung phlung* of his cross
my Savior the lonesome bundle
of this narrow land
bought with blood
the sun eating the earth
back to nothing
always nibbling the mowed fields
the worn barns
the pound of my heart
when I pass
and there's not much room
but I've been behind so long
yez the angels sing
in the winking band
we'll be changed to glory
if praise be true
how the car stumbles
over the hill
that long road he took me
more times sister than I remember
over humps
yez Jesus showed how much *luv*
there is in death.

Noli Me Tangere

Jorie Graham

1

You see the angels have come to sit on the delay
  for a while,
they have come to harrow the fixities, the sharp edges
  of this open
sepulcher,
  they have brought their swiftnesses like musics

down
  to fit them on the listening.
Their robes, their white openmindedness gliding into the corners,
  slipping this way then that
over the degrees, over the marble

flutings.
  The small angelic scripts pressing up through the veils.
The made shape pressing
  up through the windy cloth.
I've watched all afternoon how the large
  red birds here

cross and recross neither for play nor hunger
  the gaps that constitute our chainlink fence,
pressing themselves narrowly against the metal,
  feeding their bodies and wings
tightly in.
  Out of what ceases into what is ceasing.
Out of the light which holds steel and its alloys,

into the words for it like some robe or glory,
    and all of this rising up into the deep unbearable thinness,
the great babyblue exhalation of the one God
    as if in satisfaction at some right ending
come,

then down onto the dustyness that still somehow holds
    its form as downslope and new green meadow
through which at any moment
    something swifter
might cut.
    It is about to be
Spring.
    The secret cannot be

kept.
    It wants to cross over, it wants
to be a lie.

2

Is that it then? Is that the law of freedom?
    That she must see him yet must not touch?
Below them the soldiers sleep their pure deep sleep.
    Is he light
who has turned forbidding and thrust his hand up
    in fury,
is he flesh
    so desperate to escape, to carry his purpose away?
She wants to put her hands in,
    she wants to touch him.
He wants her to believe,
    who has just trusted what her eyes have given her,

123

he wants her to look away.
    I've listened where the words and the minutes would touch,
I've tried to hear in that slippage what
      beauty is—
her soil, his sweet tune like footsteps
      over the path of

least resistance. I can see
      the body composed
of the distance between them.
    I know it is ours: he must change, she must
remember.
    But you see it is not clear to me why she

must be driven back,
    why it is the whole darkness that belongs to her
and its days,
    why it is these hillsides she must become,
supporting even now the whole weight of the weightless,
    letting the plotlines wander all over her,

crumbling into every digressive beauty,
    her longings all stitchwork towards his immaculate rent,
all alphabet on the wind as she rises from prayer. . . .

3

It is the horror, Destination,
    pulling the whole long song
down, like a bad toss
    let go
in order to start again right,
    and it is wrong

to let its one inaudible note govern our going
    isn't it, siren over this open meadow
singing always your one song of shape of
    home. I have seen how the smoke here
inhabits a space
    in the body of air it must therefore displace,

and the tree-shaped gap the tree inhabits,
    and the tree-shaped gap the tree
invents. Siren,
    reader,
it is here, only here,
    in this gap

between us,
    that the body of who we are
to have been
    emerges: imagine:
she lets him go,
    she lets him through the day faster than the day,

among the brisk wings
    upsetting the flowerpots,
among the birds arranging and rearranging the shape of
    the delay,
she lets him
    slip free,

letting him posit the sweet appointment,
    letting out that gold thread that crazy melody
of stations,
    reds, birds, dayfall, screen-door,
desire,

until you have to go with him, don't you,

until you have to leave her be
    if all you have to touch her with
is form.

Breakdancing

Teresa: Saint Teresa of Avila

Staying alive the boy on the screen is doing it,
    the secret nobody knows like a rapture through his limbs,
the secret, *the robot-like succession of joint isolations*
    that simulate a body's reaction to
electric shock.
    This is how it tells itself: pops, ticks, waves and the

float. What
    is poverty for, Mr. Speed, Dr. Cadet, Dr. Rage,
Timex? Don't push me the limbs are whispering, don't push
    'cause I'm close to the edge the footwork is whispering
down onto the sidewalk that won't give in won't go some other
    where while the TV

hums and behind me their breathings, husband, daughter, too slow,
    go in to that other place and come back out
unstained, handfuls at a time, air, air—
    The flag of the greatest democracy on earth
waves in the wind with the sound turned off. The current

rubs through the stars and stripes
    like a muttering passing through a crowd and coming out an
anthem,
    string of words on its search
and destroy
   needing bodies, bodies. . . .
I'm listening to where she must not choke. I'm listening
    to where he must not be betrayed. I'm trying
to hear pity, the idiom. I'm trying to lean into those
    marshes and hear

what comes through clean,
    what comes through changed,
having needed us.
    Oh but you must not fail to eat and sleep Teresa murmurs to
her flock,

staying alive is the most costly gift you have to offer Him—all the while
                                    watching,
    (whispering Lord, what will you have me
do?) for his corporal
    appearance
in the light of the sixteenth century, in the story that flutters
    blowzy over the body of the land
we must now somehow ram
    the radioactive waste

into. He
    showed himself to her in pieces.
First the fingertips, there in mid-air,
    clotting, floating, held up by the invisible, neither rising
nor falling nor approaching nor lingering, then hands, then a

few days later feet, torso, then arms, each part alone, each part
    free of its argument, then days, then eyes,
then face entire, then days again, then *His*
    most sacred humanity in its risen form
was represented to me

completely. "Don't try
    to hold me in yourself (the air, hissing) but try to hold yourself
in me," Nov 18, 1570. I'm listening to where she must not choke,
    I'm listening to where he must not, must not. . . . Air,
holding a girl in a man's arms now,
    making them look like wind,

what if they can't be returned to you
    the *things* now reaching me—the three

exhalings, hum, blue light, the minutes, the massacres, the strict halflife
    radioactive isotopes, the shallow
graves, the seventeen rememberable personal
    lies? What if they go only this far, grounding
in me, staying
    alive?
Here is the secret: the end is an animal.
    Here is the secret: the end is an animal growing by

accretion, image by image, vote by
    vote. *No more pain* hums the air,
as the form of things shall have fallen
    from thee, no more pain, just the here and the now, the jackpot, the
watching, minutes exploding like thousands of silver dollars all over your
    face your hands but tenderly, almost tenderly, turning mid-air, gleaming
so slow, as if it could last,
    frame after frame of nowhere

turning into the living past.

Improvisation Before the Introit

James Hoggard

This time, I am certain, I should begin directly
rather than obliquely, advancing gently
but not tentatively, as I ease control,
releasing the voice flowing through me
    but trying to keep the flow limpid,
like the measured air of plainsong,
like the subtly changing colors
in the pleats of the choir robes
during the procession when descants rise
(faint bells ringing distantly in memory)
    and candle flames dance
    away the world's darkness:
the small sail-shaped fires leading us
    outside ourselves

These tones I seek are not yet mine
though they do purl through me,
rolling like rising shadowshapes
wind-buffeted gulls leave above the beach
    moments before the sinking sun dyes
the cloud-pillowed dusk red purple and gold
Then evening turns grey and breezes sweep
all the daybirds' bodies away
My god, if their auras fall now, where
(faint bells ringing distantly in memory)
    will they rise at dawn?
    There are secrets the sea
will not let one find while twilight

nurtures one's flesh
and creates one's mind

Saints whose daily lives described God
live in the shadows cast by the past
They live in the caves where the world begins
again and again in water that seeps
      through columns, through tubular walls
that wind into and out of the light
as the small sounds that echo off them
name both what we see and don't see: the walls
we wind through are labyrinthine, and on them
moisture slides then drips on pocked rocks
(faint bells ringing distantly in memory)
      but the constant light
      we pray will shine on us
comes only in glimmers, like water slowly
      pooling in the dark

In this time when congregants prepare
themselves with prayer, I trace the oak
beams whose arcs wave across our ceiling,
and through memory I see symbols in them—
      cock, lamb, fish, cedar tree, rose—
each one centered in a diamond-shaped pane
within the long aisle windows: details
set like omphaloi that give voice
to the tableaux in the altar's rose window
(faint bells ringing distantly in memory)
      and slanting keenly, eastern light
      descends upon us all:
a hushed and receptive mass now ready
      for the shepherd's crook

This music plays me more than I play it,
and if it says sometimes no past exists
it also says this world is a current of ocean
whose tide washes toward the beach
        then washes back, and wonder exists
for as long as worship lasts,
music remaking the swept world new,
placing new timbre in one's voice,
and telling us all now: Listen
(faint bells ringing distantly in memory)
        to sobering plainsong chants,
        to silence between phrases,
to the voice from the vault of the ceiling,

        for there are waves that take us now
        far away from this restive land,
                bombed, restive land,
        but back now into the broken land,
        faint bells ringing distantly in memory:
their pealing a call from a dream of a place
                where voices insist
        on justice and mercy and honor

Solvite Templum Hoc

For the dedication of the Portiuncula,
Franciscan University of Steubenville,
23 October 1987

John R. Holmes

Your parable struck lightning in the eyes
Of him whose Papal audience you sought,
For deep beneath the billows of his thought
A half-remembered dream began to rise.
The Lateran basilica he viewed,
The Temple of the New Jerusalem
Whose patrons (moneylenders, all of them)
Have set it tottering and made it crude.
But then a dirty beggar takes control,
And in a trice restores his Father's house.
A Samson in reverse, the beggar bows,
And, hands upon the pillars, holds it whole.
His Holiness now sees the dream fulfilled:
He sees in you the church you will rebuild.

Georges de la Tour:
The Penitent Magdalene
circa 1640

David Brendan Hopes

Folded to mark a page never returned to,
you find a picture of yourself
       walking among sunflowers.
A blue cap tilts back on your head,
leaving room on your brow for a slash of light
brash enough to throw the balance off,
a wayward brightness capturing the eye
       which for an instant holds all wisdom.
You remember the moment, the happiness
you thought would never fade,
yet which, as it turned out, never came again.
You recall the sunburst of the flowers
at your chest like lovers listening for the rhythm
of the hearts of lovers,
the white rose beating in the iron cage.
       You hold the photograph so shadow falls
upon the face, that one time beautiful,
difficult now to look upon. Whose was it really?
Was it your face before the present world?

       Say to one who happens by,
as though some apology were in order,
"Who was I to walk among sunflowers like a man?"

You take the brush and paint—
not quite frantically, not quite without purpose,
though to an onlooker

134

somewhat beyond the necessary passion.
You paint a kestrel hovering midair,
wings bent like a dove's,
with bloodier and more beautiful intent.
You paint the legend of a lover
who burst into flame
when his lady, laughing, slammed the door.
Compassion guides the clenched lines,
the shell-curve modeling of the hand
lifted to the mouth in horror.
You paint how he burned for seven hours,
standing straight up, arms outstretched,
Jove-bolted tree of two sad branches
shivered suddenly to scarlet flower.
How she, fleeing into farther rooms,
still saw the flicker on the wall,
still his green eyes unconsumed
amid the leaping gold, through any curtain,
through clenched hands and wet lids of her eyes.

On a day of no particular distinction,
and she no longer young.

Wait for the critics to sift through flames
to the ash of stately consummation.
They will praise details:
The miniature on the lady's wall,
in which the princess
falls among the dragons.
In the painting's window, clear and small,
a mantis snags a blown leaf with her
saw-tooth arms, bites the pointless gold,
swiveling her green head toward starvation.

Use what you have.
Of the rest, assume the worst.

As in De La Tour's *The Penitent Magdalene*, less obvious
effects make epics in a little:
the bracelets orphaned in the shadow at her feet,
the rope of pearl whose paleness
            balances the paleness of a skull.
The pearl has changed its metaphor
from frippery to a Kingdom,
nature unspecified but of great price.
            A woman gazes through a mirror
at the black behind the mirror.

A woman in a red dress in the great darkness
of the world. One candle.

            The zig-zag of the red dress
is a stairway—steep, broken—
she has mounted half way up.
            Genius here is to reveal
nothing in the mirror, nothing that she sees
but flame in flesh tone, leaping.
The flame burns opposite the heart
            in the saint's uncovered breast:
a juxtaposition, as if accidental,
of the candle like a full moon
burning sweat and perfume from the tousled room.
It is the exterior image of a heart.
            In flame-tone it roars up.
Or is poised to roar in this instant
of final, agonized repose.
Before that instant when you realize there is no mirror
but your own eyes into which the saint's eyes
terribly descend.

Saint Mary Red Dress!
you might cry into the quiet,
thinking should she turn to see her torment
in the gilt black crystal of your face,
should she mate her heart with your heart,
        you might catch flame,
comet-like take flight on red pinions
that are the lead weights of your passions
        all transformed,
lift on them finally,
unquenchable, larking
in a cloud of squandered ointment
        out from these penitential rooms and over.

A Passion Play

Easter rises from the plain of days
like Binns Crest from its skirt of cows.
Here are the low hills that have stared
into our windows like a mad uncle
since the first thing we remember.
Here is our perfectible little town,
our historic Main Street, our Founder's Elm
saved from blight at great expense.
Here is Kiwanis Park with its green benches,
its white wedding cake gazebo.
This is the make-shift stage
sweet with sawn wood.
This is the Passion Play.
The bleachers are full, not merely with our own,
but with folks from Lisbon and across the river,
in the lot a license plate from Indiana.
Same story always, but the players change.
Now behind the rope-and-blanket curtain,
high school track coach Lord Christ
ties his blond hair back with Nazarene simplicity.
The Queen of Heaven folds her apron for a day,
counting not the lost tips, but bearing witness
by breast-curve, by leap of thighs
to God among the bleachers.
Magdalene's children gawk from the shade
of the Cola sign, their mother changed before them,
her cloud hair floating on the wind.

I wondered what I'd be this year.
Not fierce Christ in these merchant's bones,
surely, nor the man-storm Peter,
not Herod, Caiphas, the villains

138

whose dedication astonishes even the saints.
Not Judas, sympathetic in the modern way,
by mad Israel tormented,
by the dawdling Incarnation
driven to desperate acts.
As a child I was the last, mute angel.
I hoped at best for the Centurion Who Believed,
the sleepy guard pillowed on Christ's coat,
Nicodemus who is troubled at night
and goes dangerously to see the Master,
who thinks God might raise a prophet if He please,
even from the middle of Galilee.

But they said, **You, John.**
The beginning was that word.
After a few rehearsals in my dusty robe,
a few splinters through my sandals
I became Christ's beloved,
who in the paintings leans in closest.
It was glory walking with him.
Pharisees bent to their books, rebuked.
Rich men snipped the bangles from their clothes.
I danced a little in my walk
to walk so with a god who loved me.

Then there was nothing but raw crossed wood,
a wrecked man willing me a mother,
all crushed and weeping worse than in the script.
Our voices skittered down the grass
like flushed birds, tinny, husky, gone.
The crowd behind me holds its breath.
I want to turn to them
from this intolerable tableau
and say **children.**

My story comes after this.
John, Apostle, Saint John Gospel-Maker,
Eagle of the Most High, John of the Apocalypse
weeps here on a wooden plank, my Lord
bleeding between two sticks,
the Holy City yet unseen,
floating bright Jerusalem mothering her beasts
and angels in the Lamb's white fleece forever,
flame, a gulf of fire, a city on Binns Crest
templed with the sun and moon.

Three minutes on the stage means three days.
East of us, a light.
This is poor John at the empty tomb.
I know what is coming.
I grip my beard in my two hands and laugh.
I must run to tell the others.

Jumping Jack

Four fury colors the jumping jack chose:
black-red for bearing,
gold for the kiss,
rose-blue for murder,
white in bliss.
White bursts the apple, red-black the rose,
three stones on the heart-bone
jumping jack knows.

Blood scrubs the apple whiter than rose.
Fox frees the heart-bone:
Sun's gold it goes.
Three prickly blossoms the fire-sprung chose:
Jack in the bramble   Fox in the rose.

The Cestello Annunciation

Andrew Hudgins

The angel has already said, *Be not afraid.*
He's said, *The power of the Most High*
will darken you. Her eyes are downcast and half closed.
And there's a long pause—a pause here of forever—
as the angel crowds her. She backs away,
her left side pressed against the picture frame.

He kneels. He's come in all unearthly innocence
to tell her of glory—not knowing, not remembering
how terrible it is. And Botticelli
gives her eternity to turn, look out the doorway, where
on a far hill floats a castle, and halfway across
the river toward it juts a bridge, not completed—

and neither is the touch, angel to virgin,
both her hands held up, both elegant, one raised
as if to say *stop,* while the other hand, the right one,
reaches toward his; and, as it does, it parts her blue robe
and reveals the concealed red of her inner garment
to the red tiles of the floor and the red folds

of the angel's robe. But her whole body pulls away.
Only her head, already haloed, bows,
acquiescing. And though she will, she's not yet said,
Behold, I am the handmaid of the Lord,
as Botticelli, in his great pity,

lets her refuse, accept, refuse, and think again.

Heat Lightning in a Time of Drought

My neighbor, drunk, stood on his lawn and yelled,
Want some! Want some! He bellowed it as cops
cuffed him, shoved him in their back seat—*Want some!*—
and drove away. Now I lie here awake,
not by choice, listening to the crickets' high
electric trill, urgent with lust. Heat lightning flashes.
The crickets will not, will not stop. I wish
that I could shut the window, pull the curtain, sleep.
But it's too hot. *Want some!* He screamed it till
I was afraid I'd made him up to scream
what I knew better than to say out loud
although it's August-hot and every move
bathes me in sweat and we are careless,
careless, careless, every one of us,
and when my neighbor screams out in his yard
like one dog howling for another dog,
I call the cops, then lie in my own sweat,
remembering the woman
who, at a party on a night this hot,
walked up to me, propped her chin on my chest,
and sighed. She was a little drunk, the love-light
unshielded in her eyes. We fell in love.
One day at supper the light fixture dropped,
exploded on the table. Glass flew around us,
a low, slow-motion blossoming of razors.
She was unhurt till I reached out my hand
—left hand—to brush glass from her face.
Two drops of blood ran down her cheek.
On TV, I'd seen a teacher dip a rose
in liquid nitrogen. When he withdrew it,
it smoked, frozen solid. He snapped one petal, frail
as isinglass, and then, against the table,

he shattered it. The whole rose blew apart.
Like us. And then one day the doorbell rang.
A salesman said, *Watch this!* He stripped my bed
and vacuumed it. The nozzle sucked up two
full, measured cups of light gray flakes. He said,
That's human skin. I stood, refusing the purchase,
stood staring at her flesh and mine commingled
inside the measuring cup, stood there and thought,
*She's been gone two years, she's married, and all this time
her flesh has been in bed with me.* Don't laugh.
Don't laugh. That's what the Little Moron says
when he arrives home early from a trip
and finds his wife in bed with someone else.
The man runs off. The Little Moron puts
a pistol to his own head, cocks the hammer.
His wife, in bed, sheets pulled up to her breasts,
starts laughing. *Don't you laugh!* he screams. *Don't laugh—
you're next.* It is the wisest joke I know because
the heart's a violent muscle, opening
and closing. Who knows what we might do:
by night, the craziness of dreams; by day,
the craziness of logic. Listen!
My brother told me of a man wheeled, screaming,
into the ward, a large Coke bottle rammed
up his ass. I was awed: there is no telling
what we'll do in our fierce drive to come together.
The heart keeps opening and closing like a mine
where fire still burns, a century underground,
following the veins of black coal, rearing up
to take a barn, a house, a pasture. Although
I wish that it would rain tonight, I fret
about the heat lightning that flicks and glitters
on the horizon as if it promised rain.
It can't. But I walk outside, stand on parched grass,
and watch it hungrily—all light, all dazzle—

144

remembering how we'd drive out past the town's light,
sit on the hood, and watch great thunderheads
huge as a state—say, Delaware—sail past. Branched
lightning jagged, burst the dark from zenith to horizon.
We stared at almost nothing: some live oaks,
the waist-high corn. Slow raindrops smacked the corn,
plopped in the dirt around us, drummed the roof,
and finally reached out, tapped us on the shoulders.
We drove home in the downpour, laughed, made love
—still wet with rain—and slept. But why stop there?
Each happy memory leads me to a sad one:
the friend who helped me through my grief by drinking
all of my liquor. And when, at last, we reached
the wretched mescal, he carefully sliced off
the worm's black face, ate its white body, staggered
onto this very lawn, and racked and heaved
until I helped him up. *You're okay, John.*
You've puked it out. "No, man—you're wrong. That worm
ain't ever coming out." Heat lightning flashes.
No rain falls and no thunder cracks the heat.
No first concussion dwindles to a long
low rolling growl. I go in the house, lie down,
pray, masturbate, drift to the edge of sleep.
I wish my soul were larger than it is.

Christ As a Gardener

The boxwoods planted in the park spell LIVE.
I never noticed it until they died.
Before, the entwined green had smudged the word
unreadable. And when they take their own advice
again—come spring, come Easter—no one will know
a word is buried in the leaves. I love the way
that Mary thought her resurrected Lord
a gardener. It wasn't just the broad-brimmed hat
and muddy robe that fooled her: he was *that* changed.
He looks across the unturned field, the riot
of unscythed grass, the smattering of wildflowers.
Before he can stop himself, he's on his knees.
He roots up stubborn weeds, pinches the suckers,
deciding order here—what lives, what dies,
and how. But it goes deeper even than that.
His hands burn and his bare feet smolder. He longs
to lie down inside the long, dew-moist furrows
and press his pierced side and his broken forehead
into the dirt. But he's already done it—
passed through one death and out the other side.
He laughs. He kicks his bright spade in the earth
and turns it over. Spring flashes by, then harvest.
Beneath his feet, seeds dance into the air.
They rise, and he, not noticing, ascends
on midair steppingstones of dandelion,
of milkweed, thistle, cattail, and goldenrod.

146

Identifying the Fire

Jean Janzen

Sometimes at night it blooms
in our heads like marigolds
and cock's comb in the cooling garden,

a flare at the end of a long lane
where the ruts finally meet.
Lover's Lane where my sister and I

carried our dolls, covering
their faces. Lips like fire,
someone said, and we felt a rope

sizzling inside. Our Sunday School teacher
said it was the Holy Ghost hovering,
beating its wings over us

so that every body cell would glow.
All our years a fire consuming,
giving itself away.

We pass it on to our children,
our voices full of love and warnings,
like our own mothers bringing

mustard and tea in the feverish dark,
their hands both soothing and electric.
Even in old age they cradle

a burning as they lean
over pots of geraniums and break off
the stems to help them bloom.

All night the petals scatter
over them, and they stir as though
toward another, someone who once

entered them. A time out of time
kindling the next breath,
and at its far end, branches, gesturing.

Facets

All the way from the Nickel-Back cafe
past the college to home,
the block of ice shimmered
in its growing puddle.
The wagon wheels stirred up the hot dust
of September. Now father slides it
into the icebox. Thud of the door,
sighs as he leans once more over the Doctrine
of Christ and the required genetics.
Fifty, already gray, he has brought us
on his journey of learning.
To know the truth, to hold it up
and examine it, like sun on crystal.
This is the year I turn thirteen,
the year of my catechism:
What are the attributes of God,
the five steps to salvation?
The sun spins over the men's dorm
where we live, scorches the elms,
clamors against the windowpanes.
At night cicadas drill their urgencies
and the college men shout and gallop
on the stairs. I can hardly hear
my own heart, its din of voices calling
to my father to rescue me
from the baptismal waters.
In the shadowed kitchen he is bending
over books, and drop by drop the ice
redefines itself in the dark.

Plain Wedding

I try to imagine my grandparents
on their wedding day flying
over the Russian village
with cow and moon. But Chagall's donkey
drops them with a thump.
None of that frivolity,
the fathers said. Black dress
for the bride, like penance
over the apple-breasts.
Hair tightly bound.

What could have lifted them
above the somber wedding sermon
and congregation was song,
that sturdy vine which creeps
and thrusts into the barest room.
Warm voices in four parts
lifting the four corners of paradise
with its lavendar skies.
"Grosser Gott, Wir Loben Dich"
washing over them, a purity
of canvas, of bride. Not to be
blemished, but with touch
upon touch, to be filled.

Flowers of Amsterdam

For the sake of the Gospel,
the book says. 1549. Pieter, Johann
and Barbara are tied to the stake.
Their bodies flare out in a triple bloom,
still flare out in the mind, the recalcitrant
flesh still acrid. And Catherine drowns
in the canal, her skirts billowing out
over her tied legs like a lily.

Now vast markets of flowers, a harbor
where once a shipload of grain
was exchanged for a single tulip bulb.
City of night when the streets open
their black laps for the painted blooms,
when music rides the blue and swollen veins,
washed and languid houses that double
in the watery streets.

City of choices. Which fire, which perfume,
and at what price? Catherine cries out
over the water. Each one must choose,
she calls into our bright throats,
each one for himself. And how
do you choose when a whirlpool sucks you in,
into the purple corridors of the iris,
the cool swarm of apple orchards?
"Careful of the feast's tomorrow," Van Gogh
writes near the end, after the yellow skies.
"For my own work I am risking my life,
and my mind is half-gone . . . But what do you want?"

What do you want? The one way to live,
the one unequivocal rose in this life
of mirrors, in this city of water where
the day is now nearly gone and the floodgates
already open. The dark elms dip their hair
into the rising tide and the laden boats
drift with the current. But here and there
one moves against it, one figure in a boat,
the twin oars quietly opening the water's
glistening petals, opening a secret passage
in the deep and watery place.

Ascension of the Red Madonna

For Michael Kane

Mark Jarman

She's been gone whenever I looked
and here photographed black and white
she's leaving, as good as gone.
Blurred wings hoist her canopy,
black of course as if black
folded all colors into its cloak.
Above the canvas, white,
the rainbow's egg, waits to be filled in
burning in arc brisé windows.

She never rose in my life
but the tearlessness of this act
is a catechism of joy. Arms
flung up to her, everyone wants
what she wants, for her to be gone,
out of the world, out of those
flamboyant windows where light,
the photographer's blinded plate,
appearing as nothing is everything.

Last Suppers

Loneliest when hung in a church annex,
Like a No Smoking sign, itself ablaze.
In the faithful reproductions the deterioration
Hangs like religious haze in the Upper Room.

Times I have noticed it was present fix
And obliterate the rooms where it was hung.
The scene so intimate in its dismay,
Familiar as a family's daily warfare.

What has happened? It's as if dinner has ended
With Father drunk again and Mother silent.
The daughters are enlisted to clean up.
They leave. And the sons begin to fight.

But, no. Christ has forecast his betrayal.
The group gesticulates, the traitor shrinks,
Spilling the salt for bad luck. And the meal
Is not finished, still has to be eaten.

*

I knew a family who hung a Last Supper
Above their dining table. A box of glass,
Like an aquarium of fish and weed,
With a lightbulb to turn the colors on.

I don't have to picture them together.
I've sat in their bitter circle, underneath
The lit-up masterpiece, heartsick, knowing
Dessert was the old man's fist against his eldest

And down the punching order to my friend.
Septic with unshed tears, he would turn on me,
And yet not bring himself to raise his fist.
His younger sister would stand up on a chair,

As Jesus and his apostles were switched off,
And point and say, "That's God." You had to answer
Before the scene went dark. You had to say,
"Yes," to her catechism. "That is God."

*

A child, I was brought into a room,
Geometrical with shadows, in Milan,
And a chill like an embrace from underground.
Our silence was a reverence for a picture.

There was the great painting behind a rope
And a parental awe I couldn't share.
I was impressed by the museum photograph
Of the bombed church and the story of survival.

The copy that we bought was done on silk.
As precious as a prayer shawl, it would hang
Beside my father's desk at church, its colors
Ancient in the fluorescent, humming light.

Alone once, going through his desk, I found
Capsules of ammonia in silk sacks,
Aids for someone who dealt with the poor in spirit,
Cracked one, and felt my head snap back.

*

The irony and genius of the thing
Is that it does not look at us. The foreground
Figures are obsessed with one another.
A landscape watches them through distant windows.

Everywhere it appears, in books, in rooms,
The painting turns its subjects toward their Lord
And one another. Their gestures sing a hymn
Of self-importance. And he averts his eyes.

On our side, the world runs through its days
Or, if you wish, it braids in endless spirals.
And what we occupy and set in motion
Jars or meshes. When we pause to look outside,

Pictures look back at us and words respond,
Images return our human gaze.
But this, despite the copying, resists.
What matters is the loneliness of God.

*

Everyone knows the silence like a wind
You have to crouch in to eat your food in safety,
Or the outburst that rains poison on the supper,
Or dining alone, in your room or with a book.

Mother coming to the table piping hot
And Father on the rocks cranky with bourbon.
The children sensing the collision coming,
Sullen themselves, urging it to happen.

The reaction could as easily take place
While getting in the car or getting out,
Around the Christmas tree or television.
All it needs is a family's critical mass.

And yet the table is a raft to cling to.
Becalmed, each pins down an unsteady edge.
And when the swell, anger, rolls through the meal,
The inner cry is "Save yourself, if you can!"

*

I have a memory of Passover,
Crackling with an air of irritation.
We feared Elijah would enrage the host,
If he appeared at all, by being late.

To put our figures back into that evening,
The young couples, the parents, the empty chair,
Risks the restorer's bungling that can hasten
Collapse. Better to say, "We ate together."

And not that one kept looking at his plate.
One drank several glasses of sweet wine.
There was a moment nobody would speak.
Two fell out of love across the table.

Now the scene only retains its lines.
Color and character—the eyes, for example—
Are lost in clouds of crumbled memory.
Whole areas—the room, the year—have vanished.

*

The tumult of the twelve thrusts out a snaking
Embrace to clutch us close and feel the pressure
Of our belief or nonbelief. It pulls,
In either case, the eye close to the faces.

And most of them are marred beyond belief.
They fade in the pointillism of decay,
Like blown-up newspaper photography.
What moves us in the remnants? Common pathos.

Leonardo set the catastrophe in motion
By giving himself time to work slowly,
Thus mixed a base that let him perfect details.
In making the picture right he made it mortal.

Most copies restore exact lines and colors,
Unsubtly, like parade floats or modern
Translations of translations of the Bible.
But the crudest replica can smell of blood.

*

In the original the decay is like a smoke cloud
Materializing from the walls and ceiling.
Someone, by now, should have called out, "Fire!"
And someone has, the calm one, at the center.

He has said it sadly, "Fire," and those hearing
Confer among themselves and make petitions
To ascertain if the announcement's really true.
Looked at thus they look ridiculous.

But as the smoke clears, they're not what I see,
Seized in their poses by a passion's heat.
I see a family's uninspired tableau,
Touched for once by a deep tranquillity.

They link hands, close eyes, pass a loving pressure,
Safe from disasters only God and Art
Would call down on their heads. When their eyes open,
They eat and drink and talk, at ease, in peace.

Loving Is the Worst of Christian Weather

William Jolliff

Today good Sister Esther slipped
crossing our joining gardens. She needed
to tell Faith again that rain's depressing—
that it makes her think of her ex-husband,
the fisherman. She doesn't discern that Faith
can hardly bear her, but is just habitually good.

Esther's mud on the kitchen rug doesn't
matter, either. Faith will mop again
when the kids take naps. But she'll own no reading
time today—no flight alone in clear blue spaces,
no Menno Simons, no Eberhard Arnold,
no Hutterians, no Bruderhof. Instead,

between the sink and floor, between her knees
and the linoleum, she'll suffer for home,
wish she'd been less ready for books and study,
slower to trudge amazed through Michigan snow
to feed a poet who, stunned at the wonder
of plain clothes, married her.

But Esther is powerfully depressed—her only son
has taken another fit, thinks he's God, blames her—
but it's the genes and these damn grey days.
She plies the suffering servant for coffee and talk,
and Faith pours and receives, living, for rain's
sake and a bruised heel, the sorrow of Christian weather.

160

We All Have Many Chances

Barbara Jordan

Forgiveness: a simple bandage.
This morning the sky is a manageable blue,
I hold my life to my mouth
and take it in my arms, saying nothing.
Through the window the trees change dimension
                         while I stare,
and a bird enters a corridor and disappears,
like a glove lost from a bridge.

The wind pitched hard
that day in the orchards; I flew to breathe it.
In the palm of the hill
stones pushed from the ground like molars, or
            the worn hooves of Clydesdales
uncovered from long-ago harvests.
Hornets dragged over apples, and I sat,
            for the grass grew in my joints
and I began to cry.
What will I become in this place?

I'm afraid of a wasted life, to find myself
the face behind a curtain
in an upstairs room, a dispassionate woman
watching shadows cross the lawn
and black spoons lifting among the leaves
in the evening.

The Cannibals of Autumn

Neither time's worn edges, nor violent windows
    (climbed by trickling leaves)
recall a race
that possessed no contour apart from landscape,
but just as we, if we lived roofless,
would be oppressed by an orchard darkness
upon ourselves and our appliances.
                And the strangled wisteria,
vagrant at the back door, autumn after autumn
as we grow suspicious, cling to our reflections
like lizards of prayer.

I've walked through the city of gargoyles, Paris,
where drops and torrents
erode those prolonged mouths, the way blood is
    wished for in words.
What surprise is it, then, that sounds
catch in basins
on windy days that shake all contemplation
blowing boxes on the water.

The Waterbury Cross

X. J. Kennedy

Fall. You're driving 84 southwest—
A hillock scarlet as a side of beef
Accosts your eyes. Gigantic on its crest,
An outstretched cross stands waiting for its thief.

Your fingers as though hammered to the wheel
Clench hard. Frost-kindled sumac blazes down
Like true gore pouring from a bogus crown.
The earth grows drizzled, dazzled, and bedrenched.

Did even Wallace Stevens at the last,
Having sown all his philosophe's wild oats,
Gape for the sacred wafer and clutch fast
To Mother Church's swaddling petticoats?

Connecticut's conversions stun. Is there
Still a pale Christ who clings to hope for me,
Who bides time in a cloud? Choking, my car
Walks over water, across to Danbury.

Twilight: After Haying

Jane Kenyon

Yes, long shadows go out
from the bales; and yes, the soul
must part from the body:
what else could it do?

The men sprawl near the baler,
too tired to leave the field.
They talk and smoke,
and the tips of their cigarettes
blaze like small roses
in the night air. (It arrived
and settled among them
before they were aware.)

The moon comes
to count the bales,
and the dispossessed—
Whip-poor-will, Whip-poor-will
—sings from the dusty stubble.

These things happen . . . the soul's bliss
and suffering are bound together
like the grasses. . . .

The last, sweet exhalations
of timothy and vetch

go out with the song of the bird;
the ravaged field
grows wet with dew.

Staying at Grandma's

Sometimes they left me for the day
while they went—what does it matter
where—away. I sat and watched her work
the dough, then turn the white shape
yellow in a buttered bowl.

A coleus, wrong to my eye because its leaves
were red, was rooting on the sill
in a glass filled with water and azure
marbles. I loved to see the sun
pass through the blue.

"You know," she'd say, turning
her straight and handsome back to me,
"that the body is the temple
of the Holy Ghost."

The Holy Ghost, the oh, oh . . . the *uh*
oh, I thought, studying the toe of my new shoe,
and glad she wasn't looking at me.

Soon I'd be back in school. No more mornings
at Grandma's side while she swept the walk
or shook the dust mop by the neck.

If she loved me why did she say that
two women would be grinding at the mill,
that God would come out of the clouds
when they were least expecting him,
choose one to be with him in heaven
and leave the other there alone?

While We Were Arguing

The first snow fell—or should I say
it flew slantwise, so it seemed
to be the house
that moved so heedlessly through space.

Tears splashed and beaded on your sweater.
Then for long moments you did not speak.
No pleasure in the cups of tea I made
distractedly at four.

The sky grew dark. I heard the paper come
and went out. The moon looked down
between disintegrating clouds. I said
aloud: "You see, we have done harm."

Things

The hen flings a single pebble aside
with her yellow, reptilian foot.
Never in eternity the same sound—
a small stone falling on a red leaf.

The juncture of twig and branch,
scarred with lichen, is a gate
we might enter, singing.

The mouse pulls batting
from a hundred-year-old quilt.
She chewed a hole in a blue star
to get it, and now she thrives . . . .
Now is her time to thrive.

Things: simply lasting, then
failing to last: water, a blue heron's
eye, and the light passing
between them: into light all things
must fall, glad at last to have fallen.

Shotputters and Discus Throwers

"And if a person does not care
to transfer those terms that he learned
from lower and less worthy things
to those sublime entities."
—Saint Augustine

Leonard Kress

Cut down to size by distance, always consigned
for everybody's safety to outer fields
far from hurdlers, sprinters, vaulters, quarter
milers who—unlike us who put
the shot or spin the discus—disavow
the soul's existence. Why else would they push
their trimmed and sinewy corporeality

against the grade school lesson of parables?
But we so mired by the bulk of flesh
and muscle, forgoing assembly honors
and applause to bow and crouch inside
the lime-drawn circle that circumscribes
our earthly life—we know that everything
is only practice, imperfect imitation

of training loops eternally projected
in locker rooms of the mind. For as
the discus thrower pivots, triply, hugging
the limits of his circle, as conscious of
his former fouls, his current propensity
as Augustine—he knows it is the finger's
final flick that makes the discus soar,

all else just preparation. Just as the grunting
shotputter knows, eyeing the sad arc
of the cast iron ball, heavy and black as a soul
full of the charred ballast of neophyte
desire, that oafish humility and not
swift grace is a proper stance for heaving *that weight*
without weight, above all things that can be measured.

Mennonite Hills in Central Pennsylvania

The fat sheep drift across the ridge
Slower than the darkness.
A trail of barks makes them a mass
By circling round and round,
Spinning it like a pedal-pumped wheel,
So sheep clump singly off.

Hurled in drowsy slowness, and upended,
Flapping their whittled legs,
They slide like bashful children, unyielding
To the board, through the gate
Into the pen—without a farmer
Or his son to inspect.

They say (those prodigals who rushed off,
Lured into the world
Only to return) Sometimes the Way
To the Kingdom doesn't so much
Open up in front of you,
As close in right behind.

What He Is Missing

Peter LaSalle

St. Francis Xavier lies
On display in Old Goa; to this day
He rests in a silver, glass-topped coffin
In an empty yellow church.

A toe is gone (in 1554 a proper
Portugese lady there gnawed
That off while pretending to kiss
The corpse's weary feet, quite discreet).

Later the right hand, amputated to the elbow,
Went directly to Rome, then the rest
Up to the shoulder sent from mission to
Jesuit mission, throughout the East.

But I am here to tell you that
Despite all that, in his faded red vestments
He doesn't look too bad, and of course the giving
Never stops: love is as simple as roused doves.

P.S. In 1902 the toe showed up (strange); you may
Visit it now at the Castle of the Family Xavier, in Spain.

Ciudad Acuña

Let me have this forever
And then some: sitting in the park
One warm, bruised-blue October Saturday night
In this grittily beautiful border town
And watching my two adult sisters
Stand in line for Communion over there in
The buttery light of the big church across the street.
(They have come down from Rhode Island
To visit me in Texas, now that our mother has died,
And we took this drive for the weekend:
They made me ask around in my broken Spanish
If there was a six-o'clock Mass.)
Let the church doors be wide open like this
To the very souls of us Others, the lost ones lingering,
Now that the lovers and the vendors
And the old domino players are gone from the park, darkened;
Let Grace come softly
Through the stink of open sewage and truck exhaust,
Let it lap around the statues of
The honored heroes of the República, and the massive trees
With their trunks whitewashed so bright lower down.

East Austin

Palm Sunday, and look at how
The Mexican children have woven
The yellow-green strands into
Perfect crosses, the young priest in red
Stands on the steps of Cristo Rey
Greeting his fleeing flock;
Because soon in the backyards of those
Tiny pastel houses not much more than shacks
Strong boys will get back to work
On that Chevy clutch job, a grandmother
Will come over to share the afternoon meal
On a picnic table with a checked plastic cloth.
A conjunto tape's accordions and drums,
Lovers laughing, uncles a little beery arguing,
More hotdogs and rolls and peppered frijoles,
And the late afternoon sunlight through these
Palm trees very, very far from Gethsemane
Whispering crosses of bright on the worn cinnamon dirt.

A bony dog there scratches hard for a flea then
Returns to sleep a sleep as serious as Holy Week:
                    Redemption is near.

Prayer for the Little City

January 6

Sydney Lea

Hushed plane, the pond.   Ice-fishers' lights.   Still little city.
Men hug their whiskey   jugs inside   as they loiter among
whiffs of bait,   potbelly smoke,   sock-wool and sweat.

Laconic chat: an idle joke;   or God damn that
or God damn this,   although such words   aren't even angry,
but ordinary.   Snowmobile roads   thread our shacks

one to another;   now and then,   Big Lou throws open
his door (like an oven's,   infernal within)   and cries to a neighbor,
"Doin' some good?"   Or dirty Duane,   the one we call

"Blackfly," will call   words much the same   and the neighborhood
will rally from silence   a moment or two,   then sink back in.
It's half past ten.   Blackfly and Lou   and all the quietened

others stay through   the darkness till dawn,   whether or not
the small smelt bite.   What *of* this town,   this bobhouse crew?
What of Ben,   who's outside skimming   his ice-hole's o's?—

he sniffs and blows,   thinks vaguely of women,   and thinks to name
some part of their bodies   out loud across   the frozen surface:
a shout all worthless,   directionless,   a shout all shoddy

with platitude,   devoid of embrace,   containing nothing,
not even longing . . .   at least for sex.   Just part of a mood
and situation   much at odds,   it might be imagined,

175

with a hopeful season,   season of gods,   of resolution
to start anew.   Outside, the flags   on their planted poles
in the utter chill   are utterly slack,   betraying no

visionary   prey down under   to clasp our lures.
The dullness is pure.   No signs, no wonders,   no mystery . . .
except it be   the care with which   all night men linger,

as if in prayer   for a novel fish,   or a novel way
by which to address   some thing they're feeling.   Surely this is
part of what holds us   under crude ceilings   beaded with pitch,

amid this fetor   with speechless friends.   Surely, surely
a sense that early,   before the dawn   (or sooner, or later)
our flags will all   at once, together,   tremble and shimmy.

Epiphany   —o bright palaver!   o every hole
a yodel of steam!   So runs our fancy   in the absence of sound
in this merest of towns,   although our shanties'   very beams

of light seem bored.   O little city,   we think, it's cold;
city, how still,   how still we see thee.   Still, the stars
go by above,   even here,   and still may love

embrace the year.

Road Agent

When the sun rises, they get them away
   and lie down in their dens.
  Man goes forth to his work
   and to his labor until the evening.
—*Psalm 104*

It doesn't seem so cursed in summer.
If a job could ever turn sweet, that's when.
There's just a little brush to tend.
Or I cuff the washboard flat with the grader.

You don't even have to swat the flies.
Diesel-smoke and noise will drive them.
The best is, I can look to the mountain!
The seat will raise a man that high.

The plow's high, too, but you can't look off.
Sun-up to sun-down, eyes on the road.
The mountain's still there when it goes cold.
But in winter you have to mind yourself.

Your help will quit you sure as Judas.
I clear the ice and snow on my own.
Everyone seems to go to den.
Kiss them good-bye when the weather freezes.

They call on the town or move to the city.
It's soft, but it isn't by Jesus *my* way.
I'm not like the state boys out on the highway.
I don't despise what isn't easy.

I'm what I was made, and nothing else.
I mean to earn my bread by sweat.
Foolish, the things that some expect.
God helps them that help themselves.

Some can't dream why I'd keep at it.
No matter, what this one and that one say.
They vote me back on town meeting day.
But the new folks' notions and mine are different.

(The oldtimers don't much like to talk.
I do it for them—I'm elected.
It comes with the work, and I guess it's
The newcomers squawk and I squawk back.

First thing to do, they say, is the schoolyard.
They have to get at the books, those kids!
(True, it's what my mother said.
The times would pass me by, she figured.)

But someone should bless the poor in school.
Everyone better not turn out bright.
They do, and these roads close down tonight.
They could own the world and lose their souls.

That's in a book, and makes some sense.
I graduated with less than I brought.
Of course I started going with Hat.
You couldn't call it a total loss.

We've kept on going, with six good children.
Say *that* for some that study college.
Say they got *that* out of all their knowledge.
Say they got it from education.

Last week I was working Sutter's Knoll.
I came on poor young Mrs. Grayson.
She had this little flimsy dress on.
You'd judge she was out for a summer stroll.

Her husband's diplomas would fill a trunk.
(Half-bare, she was, in a foot of snow!
I pretended a wing was loose on the plow.)
He's one of those jacket-and-necktie drunks.

Town Hall's the next that's got to be done.
The politicians insist on that.
They're damned important, you can bet.
I guess I oughtn't to run them down.

They hang on tougher than lots of others.
Take what few are left in The Grange.
It seems so quick, the way it's changed!
There aren't that many around to remember.

Things were different here one time.
The Grange is ready to fall on the ground.
Who cares nowadays in town?
I do it early, all the same.

Let them fire me: I've lived through worse.
It wasn't Happily-Ever-After.
It wasn't Everyone-Love-Your-Neighbor.
And the good Lord knows the money was scarce.

Then I plow the American Legion Post.
(There was always a battle or two somewhere.)
Schooling, politics and war.
Father, Son, and Holy Ghost.

I'm not even supposed to do the church.
That road is twisty, even in light.
I wait and fuss with it in the night.
Taxpayer money—they'd moan and bitch.

Dead last, this house of God out here.
But He says from the mountain, The last will be first.
In the end He says, The first'll be last.
This is the one I fight to get clear.

The hardest one, in the cold of the year.

Midway

*. . . He asked him, "Do you see anything?" And he looked up and said, "I see men; but they
look like trees, walking." Then again he laid hands upon his eyes; and he looked intently,
and was restored, and saw everything clearly.*
—*Mark 8:23-25*

January.
The hours after midday are coming
back, there is time
to climb from home
to height of land for the broader vision:
north and east,
Mount Moosilauke,
its four rivers of snow conjoining;
directly west,
the little town
on the highway, all its citizens
without a doubt
preoccupied
with matters they find as grave as any;
and all around,

the traffic of beasts,
invisible now, great and tiny.
A pregnant jumble,
near and far,
then and now, in a time of year
stormy and frigid,
but I have sweated,
stripped to the waist, it has been so clear.
The dead have been dead
it seems so long,
and yet their ghosts are perched on every

branch above me,
cloaking themselves
in the rising vapors from my body,
the day's sole clouds.

Deep in the Sunday
village, forlorn, the sound of swings
in the empty schoolyard
clinking against
their cold steel standards, like diminished
steeple bells:
ten o'clock's
sparse service was over hours
ago. My father
lays hands on my sight
up here, and friends, and my furious brother,
who at last seems calm.
The night is losing
its sovereignty, it will not be
overlong

before it loses
its winter boast, "Come out with me,
come out and stay,
and you'll be a corpse."
The crickets, partridge, frogs will all
come back to drum
their victory;
the whippoorwills will make their hum
and click as they mate,
the freshets will loosen;
the children, done for the year with lessons,
will elect to throng
the grassy playground. . . .

The past will turn itself over, shaking
out my brother,

friends, and father,
and they will be as before, but better,
as I will be,
unless—as so often—
I'm dreaming here; unless what I sense
is just another
misty version
of lifelong longing. It's hard to say . . . .
A moment ago,
I flushed a crowd
of flying squirrels, who in their soaring
looked so like angels
I rubbed my eyes. And what do I see?
On the far horizon

appears to be
a line of men, there in procession . . .
as darkness deepens, they look like trees.

Gethsemani Abbey
Kentucky
(remembering)

J. T. Ledbetter

From Merton's hermitage I watched
the Abbey fade in the dusk
where monks blended in the shadows
of the crows circling above iron trees.
The Kentucky knobs humped on the horizon
like knuckles, and I thought of my father
on the farm in Illinois, watching his maples
fade into the same night, waiting for me.

And I thought of the day before,
when my Aunt Emma opened her book
on Revelation and praised God for it
and for the T.V. ministry,
and looked me in the eye
and asked if I was saved.

Then there was the business of the 21 shrimp
my father said we had to get at Carlyle Lake
on Tuesday night because that's the only time
you got the 21
otherwise it was something like 12
and then not with the cole slaw.

So we drove through the warm night,
my father silhouetted in the blue dash light
hungry to please me,

talking of woods,
how it was time to come home.
And I caught his eyes in the mirror,
thinking of my plane waiting in the darkness
like my aunt's fiery cherubim with their wings
covering their feet.

The Tide

Denise Levertov

Where is the Giver to whom my gratitude
rose? In this emptiness
there seems no Presence.

*

How confidently the desires
of God are spoken of!
Perhaps God wants
something quite different.
Or nothing, nothing at all.

*

Blue smoke from small
peaceable hearths ascending
without resistance in luminous
evening air.
Or eager mornings—waking
as if to a song's call.
Easily I can conjure
a myriad images
of faith.
Remote. They pass
as I turn a page.

*

Outlying houses, and the train's
   rhythm
slows, there's a signal box,
People are taking their luggage
down from the racks.
Then you wake and discover
you have not left
to begin the journey.

*

Faith's a tide, it seems, ebbs and flows responsive
to action and inaction.
Remain in stasis, blown sand
stings your face, anemones
shrivel in rock pools no wave renews.
Clean the littered beach, clear
the lines of a forming poem,
the waters flood inward.
Dull stones again fulfill
their glowing destinies, and emptiness
is a cup, and holds
the ocean.

On a Theme by Thomas Merton

'Adam, where are you?'
                      God's hands
palpate darkness, the void
that is Adam's inattention,
his confused attention to everything,
impassioned by multiplicity, his despair.

Multiplicity, his despair;
                      God's hands
enacting blindness. Like a child
at a barbaric fairgrounds—
noise, lights, the violent odors—
Adam fragments himself. The whirling rides!

Fragmented Adam stares.
                      God's hands
unseen, the whirling rides
dazzle, the lights blind him. Fragmented,
he is not present to himself. God
suffers the void that is his absence.

Salvator Mundi: Via Crucis

Maybe He looked indeed
much as Rembrandt envisioned Him
in those small heads that seem in fact
portraits of more than a model.
A dark, still young, very intelligent face,
a soul-mirror gaze of deep understanding, unjudging.
That face, in extremis, would have clenched its teeth
in a grimace not shown in even the great crucifixions.
The burden of humanness (I begin to see) exacted from Him
that He taste also the humiliation of dread,
cold sweat of wanting to let the whole thing go,
like any mortal hero out of his depth,
like anyone who has taken a step too far
and wants herself back.
The painters, even the greatest, don't show how,
in the midnight Garden,
or staggering uphill under the weight of the Cross,
He went through with even the human longing
to simply cease, to not be.
Not torture of body,
not the hideous betrayals humans commit
nor the faithless weakness of friends, and surely
not the anticipation of death (not then, in agony's grip)
was Incarnation's heaviest weight,
but this sickened desire to renege,
to step back from what He, Who was God,
had promised Himself, and had entered
time and flesh to enact.
Sublime acceptance, to be absolute, had to have welled
up from those depths where purpose
drifted for mortal moments.

Contraband

The tree of knowledge was the tree of reason.
That's why the taste of it
drove us from Eden. That fruit
was meant to be dried and milled to a fine powder
for use a pinch at a time, a condiment.
God had probably planned to tell us later
about this new pleasure.
                                      We stuffed our mouths full of it,
gorged on *but* and *if* and *how* and again
but, knowing no better.
It's toxic in large quantities; fumes
swirled in our heads and around us
to form a dense cloud that hardened to steel,
a wall between us and God, Who was Paradise.
Not that God is unreasonable—but reason
in such excess was tyranny
and locked us into its own limits, a polished cell
reflecting our own faces. God lives
on the other side of that mirror,
but through the slit where the barrier doesn't
quite touch ground, manages still
to squeeze in—as filtered light,
splinters of fire, a strain of music heard
then lost, then heard again.

Ascension

Stretching Himself as if again,
    through downpress of dust
        upward, soil giving way
to thread of white, that reaches
    for daylight, to open as green
        leaf that it is . . .
Can Ascension
    not have been
        arduous, almost,
as the return
    from Sheol, and
        back through the tomb
into breath?
    Matter reanimate
        now must relinquish
itself, its
    human cells,
        molecules, five
senses, linear
    vision endured
        as Man—
the sole
    all-encompassing gaze
        resumed now,
Eye of Eternity.
    Relinquished, earth's
        broken Eden.
Expulsion,
    liberation,
        last
self-enjoined task
    of Incarnation.

He again
Fathering Himself.
   Seed-case
      splitting,
He again
   Mothering His birth:
      torture and bliss.

Before the Monstrance

Bob Lietz

I kneel on tiles at the back.
The host glows in overhead light.
Then wind we'll have for ourselves
eight months
distracts me from my prayers,
from the guitarist's chording
fetching the past's slipped notes.
Dust took on the colors
of stained glass, the motions of dust
a dumbsaying. Plainer maybe,
this could be the same parish,
the same sanguine fluting
accompanied by guitar. I listened for Spirit
as for water come to boil,
relished the sadness I put on,
at their eyes piercing through
mantillas and their fans, my eyes
riveted to Hosts after . . .

Sundays, at the edges of October,
one step follows the next
through the downed leaves. I listen
to their flattened western voices
standing out in a fine choir, calling
me in from under the last green leaves,
to patience recovered here,
not so much deferring against my will
    as ordering it finely . . .

I come slowly to the tooled front pew
and rail, the parishioners
gone now, the day's liturgy inviting
my equivalent abandon.
The additions life serves up
take on the character of praise.
I have come apart and mended here,
like a child, palm up, accepting
his allowance, counting more than
could be right. I quiet
my heart some. The misconsolations
shown plainly now, the filaments
of old revulsions burn away in me,
night-lit bulbs no longer visible
in the wash of stronger light.

Retreat

I taste the fish soup, feel the cold again,
the scarcely heated northern gymnasium,
barracks sleeping. I see the ballplayers come late
from play-offs almost won.

Winter ending in a pivot year,
I watch the faces of boys my age
who hope to graduate,

for any as scared as I am by confession,
keeping their own silence
as the priests hover, struck silent
by the fathers' harmonies and tonsures,
the invitations in their chants.

I think of the six of us trying backroads,
looking for the retreat house
in northern New York snow, the house
we stopped at set down

off a snow and gravel shoulder.
The wife called up from chores
pushed through a wall of frozen laundry,
thought hard, then measured
the way for us in rods, the directions
for us in compass points.

Say her directions worked, got us through
banked snow surviving thaw for this:
St. Joseph Coopertino. March it must have been
or early April. How many small

isolated clouds crossed then? How many
souls were washed and pinned
like wrung woolens pinned to clotheswires?

Bouillabaisse. Spare meals three days.
Even now I see the bread I knelt before
but could not swallow.

Nineteen years ago, the drawing back
from bread, our clinging, two sides
of the one coin: we packed the snow
to ice balls we hurled at each other,
negotiated the details of a conduct
out of that cold yard.

River Road

Small, too remote, not stars
but barns reduced to embers, ash.
Something moral in its own way
survives. But who'd ever want
that farm, that guilt, another spring,
forearms crossed, of controlled
burns to clarify the skirts
of a drugged country?

He tries the numbers on for size,
the long local pasts
each breathing house predicts.
His temples throb like loose
clapboards. He hears the alive
dead whispering in flare-up oak,
the bells of their first tongues,
special vinegars of sense,
their voices now, like the pass
of many feathers, like
smoke a bright child squinted at
to see through.

A face like hammered metal
haunts the limbs and foliage
shrivelled back. Time accordions
all over. But none of it
to match
laps the women spread with colors,
mittens like vestiges of wills,
none of it to match
the way he knows he'll find her,
hanging her wash nude, her mind

a vehicle his own could not
conceive, conceiving Paradisal spring
    and the gardens
        they'd have fed on.

He holds his own at the glazed curve.

    Memory, like the brush of light
or combers over stone,
    picks out high water marks,
the expressions lost to wind
    and anarchies of their physicians,
remembering the sheets hung there,
    shaken to spark the winter daylight,
and children, whole days gliding ice,
    polishing their figure-8s, counting
to birthdays checked off calendars
    with coincident feasts.

    Not these lightenings of Mozart,
these sips of something resembling fire
    from a juice glass. But polkas
roused for the Church fest, embarrassed
    genuflections. And now these winds,
snaking the gaps and open sockets,
    settings the aunts display,
his own flesh razoring woodscents,
    descending to newlyweds, intendeds,
these cardinal-quick young set circling
    the table gods departed from.

    Strange to him, as daughters now
with daughters, as stories
    they tell in better English:
How could he prepare himself

for this, these *christs* they park to watch
in watertower rusts,
  on the fenders of junked Fords
lucky men climbed from,
  this almost-love, her coalstove limp,
(like a complex gift
  the world leaves him to attend,)
and skins of ice come back
  to ponds the glacier backed from,
  clouding the mirrors
    of his changed state?

Weeknights at the Cathedral

Marjorie Maddox

Weekday evenings, I watch you
stuff soprano into boy
into choir robe
like ricotta into a shell,
faces bursting on the high A.
A priest wraps the rotten notes
about his collar,
fingers them like a rosary
till they rise, whole, smooth,
beyond the organ pipes.
Sometimes you hide in those pipes,
pop out on middle C.
Sometimes you filter through the stained glass,
jiggling the tinted cross
until your thorns slip.
Today, hunchbacked on the fourth pew,
canvassed in greys,
you kneel, a beggar woman.
I think you are praying for me.

"Even the Rocks Shall Praise Him"

Their cold, mole-grey faces jut here, there:
cliffs, streets, quarries, bottoms of fishtanks,
riverbanks, collections on cardboard.

Their mineral lungs jubilate.

Like fireworks, praises screech through hemispheres;
notes collide in splendor.

Or, like the low breath of leopards,
they hum. Quote seventeenth-century hymns.

Mount Fuji lifts its rocky cheeks,
Kilimanjaro strains toward the sun
while the carols of Mounts Blanc, McKinley, Everest
peak beyond all constellations,
vibrate every planet.

Threading the Needle

I could have done it easily but for the
tick   tick   tick   of the kitchen timer
held haughtily in your hand.
What was your hurry—
camel, needle, both on lease from Arabia and me paying?

The head was no problem,
went through quickly like stiff thread
without a nick on the nose or chin.
His neck was as pliable as a noodle.
The front hooves, padded paws—both performed admirably,
tapdancing themselves through the steel loop.

All liquid drained from the paunch,
I effortlessly rolled that through the needle's eye
while you grunted, "Impossible!
Inconceivable—a dromedarius, the single hump,
stuck for years at the opening!"

I could have done it all:
popped his mound like a boil,
poked fur through the slot with a thimble
if you'd given me a bit more time,
allowed me another second.

The Great Wheel

Paul Mariani

In the Tuileries we came upon the Great Wheel
rising gargantuan above the trees. Evening
was coming on. An after-dinner stroll, descending
by easy stages towards the river, a bridge of leaves
above us, broken here and there by street lights
coming on. Our time here nearly over, our return

home a shadow hovering. Paris, city of returns,
you said, for the pleasure of it, like the Great Wheel
looming there above us, all steel & light
& music, daredevil daunting, against the evening
sky with the tower in the distance winking. The leaves
still held firmly, the unthinkable descending

of what lay ahead undreamt of still, death descending
inevitably as the Great Wheel in its return,
(a descent first through summer's golden leaves
and then bare ruined branches), the Great Wheel
turning & returning. As then, with the all but evening
over us, our wives laughing by the entrance lights,

we rose above the mansard roofs, the trees, the lights,
lifting in a vertiginous ascent before descending,
as we chattered on against the coming on of evening,
our seat creaking in the rising wind, anxious to return
now to earth's solidities. Instead, the Great Wheel
merely sighed and lifted, stopping at the top, leaving

each of us alone now with our thoughts. The leaves
below, green, graygreen, gray, the dollhouse roofs, lights
like diamonds winking, aloof & distant, the Great Wheel
playing us, two middle-aged men, each descending
towards the Wheel's one appointed end, the Great Return
to earth, as the books all have it, come our evening.

For all our feigned bravado, we could feel the evening
over us, even as we stared down upon the blur of leaves,
our wives, our distant children, on all we would return
to, the way shipwrecked sailors search for lights
along a distant shore, as we began the last descent,
leaving the tents and Garden with its Great Wheel

to return, my dear dead friend, to the winking lights
along the boulevard, leaves lifting & descending,
as now the evening air took mastery, it & the Great Wheel.

Manhattan

For Robert Creeley

Thirty years, and the six-inch scar still there
like a blasted flower. Five beers
& five Manhattans at this Hempstead bar
& then I'm heading south with Peers & Wilbur
for a White Castle, still rambling on about
my morning Ethics test & how Aquinas avers
means can be said to justify the ends—or
is it ends means?—when they're there,
this one in studded leather staring
hard at my kelly-green *Manhattan College*
jacket. And before I know it, we're
out behind the building, under
the springtime stars, & I'm breathing harder,
trying to clear my head & remember
which my left fist is & which my right.
And then stud leather comes for me, leers
through those broken teeth of his, and in sheer
terror I tear into him as we both go down,
my fists knotted in his greasy hair,
smashing his head against the blacktop.
Then all at once it's over & through a blur
of cheers I'm downing six Manhattans more
& swimming upstreet through this nightmare
to steal a toilet sign for some stranger,
ten feet of coiled barbed wire having so far
stopped him.
              But nothing can stop Manhattan.
And halfway up razor teeth are tearing
up my leg & then I'm down. And next morning I pare
back an eyelid, pain mounting everywhere,

& try to close my fishmouth wound, & tear
past my mother out of there, & at 9:05 I glare
at Ethics Question 1, then at my bloody pants
and then at Self-loathing & old friend Fear,
both already yawning at whatever
I come up with for Questions 2 & 3 & 4.

Logic

Janet McCann

A Walt Disney white rabbit
consults its watch, continues on its way,
or run the film backward, watch Alice
rise like a cork. For rules reversed are rules:

not both and, either or,
if not, then not. The steel box
emits the answer, strands of data, given.

Admit that chaos was flawed, that we slipped in
through a hole. Alice rising. Think
the world away, curve by curve uncurling,
the whole forgivable earth, firs and train cars,
spin it to a string—

But knowledge is not feeling, neither touch.
Something the mirror cannot reverse,
can not give back, is kept in the glass-bound world . . .

If old, mathematical sunsets replace sex,
a red meadow, the mind's field to roll in.

Weeds have long since overgrown the tracks
where the locomotive used to run.
Still they bend the sun's rays,
even this deep, and under snow.

A Letter of Saint Andrew the Dancer

Howard McCord

i.

Grape, ivy, pine

    fig

        lords of the moist

        myrtle

          (belonging to Dionysus and the dead)

the wet of sex
and the great folds of the sea

The seeds of all
are by nature moist

        Thales no fool

"Does not each one of us
have the face
of one who has died?"

Shiva, lord of sleep, blue-throated,
                whose-form-is-water
The madness of birth

        Beloved.

ii.

There are exits in the land
Pausanias and the local,
            the sense

    that in the groundsurge
    of high plateaux, in the mute and sleeping
            forests

                in stone
is the coda of the dance

The markings of birds
and the organic structure
of hieroglyphs
are not distinct

    this is the vision Shiva and Dionysus allow

            demand

it is the sapience of blood
        the demand of bone

            spilled in a pattern
            cracked on the fire and read

        always reading, alert
    to the clouds, the direction
        of wind, the texture of the soil
    the attempt at totality

        Shiva and Dionysus allow

    demand.

209

iii.

The Risen Christ consumes

    in the fire

of his burning, motionless body
the dualities
      in great sanity

His sanity

    His sanity is power
    over ecstasy

  the divine madness that is the power

    of Shiva and Dionysus

who are permitted ecstasy and madness

      escape

Only the Risen Christ sanity

      consuming silently
   in a stately, measureless blur of light
unmoving

    quiet

the oppositions, consuming
without movement or action

    the dancing figures of Shiva and Dionysus.

iv.

In the calm of the forest
Christ kills the gods

                who are the energy of the world
     and the progenitors of birds
             intelligence
             and the senses

to leave a white, unforgiveable light

       in summation and everywhere

  without distinction
            the still wind of light.

v.

There is no white light but that
     which streams
       from the pine cone

              thyrsus/lingam

there is no sanity save in madness
and Christ is flesh.

            Blessed flesh and local, dancing

the world to come
  with such fruit

    and glory of sound

        the Hosannas

the screams of angels and falcons
     in exaltation,

Mary, Mother of Stars—

the immense dance purified by light
     cleansed of the shadow

          infinitely expanding

          (that life may not breed on life again

but all existence
     all alive

infinitely extending in time,

          the generations
              the treasures

     the absolute present consumed and flowering
forever

     in the still and moving

        wind and light

        of Christ.

         vi.

Above all

     the waters

        beyond the firmament

breathe and move
                in the restless

     and toiling thrust of creation,
lifted and dazzling

              and all participate
              are of

    the silent peace of the white and motionless light
and the contextured grains of earth

            the salt and wet
                reality

of the sea, the open gates

      the dance.

Faith Is a Radical Master

Walter McDonald

We touch you one by one and mumble,
words stumbling on our tongues,
stunned in your blurred living room

hours after your lab report:
a little lump, a mass of bulged,
malignant cells. Telephoned,

we've come to hold you. The ghost
who walked with mourners to Emmaus
may be in this room. We are mere mortals,

all. We don't know anything but this.
Who knows this winter drought will last?
Who swears the last blind beggar's

doomed, no spittle for his lids?
Who calls down fire from heaven
and isn't seared?

Settling the Plains

For here and for the afterlife
they worked and sang, kept time
with hymn books in both hands,
old songs of God's good grace

in a land so dry they planted
cottonseeds to prove they believed
in miracles. They buried their dead
on plains with no native stones,

deep in the earth to save them
from sandstorms that pounded
daily from the west. They prayed
for rain, the sun so dry for months

they couldn't curse. Rain fell
in floods like manna twice a year.
Like Moses, they walked across
dry land and called on God

to bless them all for doubting.
They believed whatever they put
in the dirt would live if it was
God's will and the wind blew.

Nearing the End of a Century

My great-greats claimed these acres,
trying to turn back bull-necked oxen
grazing prairie grass like pastures of heaven.
From a dugout, they watched fires burn the plains.

Now, the prairie is tamed, only the country wild,
crack houses rampant, the smoke of fire storms.
Lot's wife has company, enough salt columns
to prop the ozone. Strangers with outrageous smiles

ring our doorbell, burning to save the whale,
the elephant. Downtown, old bums have given up,
their cardboard huts collapsed. Stick figures
with sidewalk signs picket all busy intersections.

I tell my sons don't look away. In Jericho
the spies made friends with Rahab, the one whore
unemployed, laughing at the guards.
I think of Jonah watching the whale rise slowly

from the ocean, the startled sea gulls screeching.
In a desert, can bones like Nineveh live?
The Philistines gloated over blinded Samson
straining, and heard the marble columns crack.

The Old Man's Flowers

David Middleton

At evening we'd glimpse him through the trees
Before the stars appeared, his hands and knees
Deep in humus, turning up his garden,
A quiet old man, humming now and then,
A watchman long retired who still preferred
To work at night and not be overheard.
He'd toil for hours spading out tough clots
Of monkey grass and clay that clogged his plots,
Almost in despair to find so many weeds
Unplanted by his hands that crushed their seeds.
He raised his flowers for beauty, not for gain,
Delighting to call in season each new strain
Out of the mottled blossoms of the rocks—
Oxalis, fire-pink, aster, purple phlox—
The budded loam and tongue become the same
Unfolding from the night as from their name.
Then, tired and content, he'd rest in his own bed
While high in the flowering heavens overhead
Star-gardens would emerge as by design
Rooted in the dark blue humus where they shine
As whorled escapes or radiant bouquets
Dotting the blackened meadows set ablaze
By a gardener burning off as he extends
His stands of aster to their cindered ends.
And though we haven't heard him sing in years
His work-song that became the music of the spheres
Descending when he tilled the fertile rows
Of maiden space in which his seed still glows,

Sometimes at evening in silence as profound
We hear a tune well hummed above this minded ground,
This patch of starry bloom and blossomed star
By some old man who tells us what we are.

Lines for the Dormition of the Virgin

Mother of love who felt in None's full moon
The Passion of your flesh so long ago,
To starlit Chartres, Cistercian Clairvaux
You bore the thousand years of summer noon.
Then dark Cartesian dreams, disturbed at birth,
Made knowledge pure as will in pure release,
Which, in the single kingdom of your peace,
Severed the realms of heaven and the earth.
Now, power, wealth, and sex, detached, discrete,
Inside their telic hells, guilty with hate
Declare themselves an uncreated state
Too whole for you to enter or complete—
You, who woke in us a love you were denied
And rose above the flesh you glorified.

Azaleas in Epiphany

Delicate hot-pink bloom,
The first chill hint of spring,
Aflame outside my room,
What message do you bring?

Some think you self-sufficient,
Spontaneously there,
Mute matter's co-efficient,
Unfolding unaware.

But I can only deem
As holy petioles
And pedicels that teem,
Leaf-tongues and petal-scrolls.

Thus taken, in their stations,
All things are angels sent
Blazing into creation,
The Word's embodiment.

The Pleasure Principle

Raymond Oliver

Who *are* you? Why do you not let me live
As I please? And how could your caress, so rough,
Be kinder than my smooth alternative?

Your steel-brush strokes are forcing me to slough,
Daily, my fleshy growths of appetite,
But still they come; I cannot have enough

I would forever scratch my itches, light
At first, then harder at the thickened sore;
But you would give me radical delight,
Gouging my itches till I have no more.

Compline

I shape this day till I can feel its heft,
Distributing each major stress and weight
Rythmically, harmonizing what is left,

Until its form and burden, however great,
Sit lightly in my comprehension's palm—
My property and handiwork, not freight.

My good, my evil, in the senescent calm
Of evening, come to terms. I contemplate
And weigh them now, like phrases of a psalm.

Christendom

Look at the gallimaufry—hurdygurdy—
Cuckoo clock with the Holy Ghost as birdie—
Empire stoked by aged "eunuchs of God"
Where whips of flagellants and Aaron's rod
Go whirling through the fiery air, to lash
Sparks of the holy from the pyre's ash—
TV evangelist with neon grin
That flashes at the touch of cash and sin—
Makers of Saints Teresa (God's own bride)
And Charlemagne (our patron of genocide)—
Crusade, that smorgasbord of death and loot
Served with a compote of forbidden fruit—
The Sunday service station of the gloss
Dispensing sermon-gas with hymnal-sauce,
The risen Easter Bunny as wonderbread:
All this the Christian bears on heart and head,
Like Atlas with a lurching, screeching load
Laboring up the pilgrim's Heaven Road.
Only its mother, or its child, could love it.
Easy to say, with show of reason: shove it.
But if you're sick from Dachau, melanoma,
The Universal Darkness, its aroma
Of death and nothing, corpse the final clown—
This is the only medicine-show in town.
So let me shove my scrupulous distress
Up some grotto, and I'll say yes, oh yes.

Scripture Lesson

Judas, one of the chosen,
For thirty pieces sold him;
Thomas' faith was pale;
Peter, when tested, failed.
Chosen people are never
Dependable. But devils,
Madmen, the sick, the blind,
Discerned him every time.

Seventeenth-Century Gravestone for a Child

Chelmsford, Mass.

The Resurrection must take *place*,
As promises take shape in deed.
Before the years of rain erase
This slate, finally, let us read
The best these parents could afford,
To claim or tenderly imagine:
Not merely "she is with the Lord"
But "she is in her Father's mansion".

Prairie Prayer

Molly Peacock

Time rolls out like a prairie.
Do not be afraid.
The mind forms a prayer
from endless land's creed.

The straight blade horizon
is grass blades in billions,
silver slanted in the sun,
the prairie soft bullion

beyond stamp or use, unowned,
undone, unformed.
A prayer forms alone
when time undoes, unforms.

The self, like land itself,
beyond stamp or use, unowned
in its unfarmed wealth
telescopes into the mind.

Now, if the mind had fingers
it would touch its thought.
Such contact would be prayer,
an endlessness inside there.

To an Atheist in a Spiritual Crisis

Marjorie Power

You pace wrench gray office carpet,
formulating questions
about the impact of art
on *the real world*.
Your cubicle

remains on the ninth floor.
Ceiling tiles inhale
your every utterance
while you cast glances,
like nets, into the swimming street.

You fax a few
misplaced apostrophes
in my direction.
Such vulnerability
to a virtual stranger.

Next time I hold
a conch shell to my ear,
I will listen for your voice.

The Taking Down

Wyatt Prunty

Ever since the seriously ill were sent away,
The sounds, smells, even the lights have changed;
These days the doctors in the valley
Export their help up to our hospital,
Where rarely anyone walks the corridors,
Now lengthened by their emptiness,
Much the way the parking lots outside
Wait like hugely widened game boards,
Especially during the holidays,
When looking out one thinks of visitors.

After Christmas and before New Year's,
The artificial Christmas tree
Is taken down and packed away
"To avoid bad luck," Mrs. Gilbert says.
She and the other volunteers
Sit in the lobby and quietly pack
The coils of wire that, covered with green needles,
Make up the tree's ten feet of branches.
They put the ornaments in smaller boxes,
Each one sealed, labeled, and numbered
So that, next year, they may reverse themselves.

For Mrs. Gilbert, the emptied corridors
And vacant parking lots mean that her wing
Along the back, looking out into the woods
From its rounded nurses' station, lounge, and rooms,
Has cycled the healing roundabout

Of charts, nurses, and starched doctors
Into something barely graspable—
The indefinite December sky
Under which she walked once as a girl,
Hurrying home and looking side to side
Between the houses' deepening porches,
Until she bundled through her own front door,
Lights out and the hall recessively still.
She remembers sitting alone for hours.

This time of year the drive from the hospital
Stretches as the halls on Mrs. Gilbert's wing
Lengthen in the early dark that seems to stall
The backward counting days before New Year's,
After the Christmas visitors have disappeared;
So Mrs. Gilbert busies herself
A little longer in each room,
And takes some added care in overseeing
That the ornaments and artificial tree
Are packed away by proper count,
Boxes numbered and stacked in sequence,
As though matching next year's calendar
By which she will arrange her hall,
Where she walks now, checking every name,
Steering her cart as she has done for five years.

The back wheels swivel as she moves,
Leaning in a push that makes the cart
Seem heavier than it is. Nothing spills.
And her list of names, which rarely changes,
Is on top, printed new each day for her,
As if she were a silent auditor
Hired to hold some closing inventory.
Sometimes her lips move, naming a new patient.
Other times, she pauses at a vacancy

And checks the room, opening the door
And feeling a draft's subtractive touch.

From down the hall, Mrs. Henry shouts
Repeatedly, "Take Me Home! Take Me Home!"
Then, offered varieties of drink,
Answers softly, "No thank you, Dear, no thank you."
The cart backed out, the shouting starts again.
Next, Mr. Elmo, who's had a stroke:
"I feel so stupid," he says, shaking his head,
"I'm dead because I'm stupid."
She offers him his cup; he looks away.
Later, when she checks, the cup's still full.

Mrs. Nicholas plays the radio all day.
She cannot use her hands to change the station
But doesn't mind, she says, because
She only wants the human voices going on.
Her friend across the hall, Mrs. Austin,
Has lost the use of her two good hands also.
She leans away, then whispers, "Are you a Christian?"
Surprised, Mrs. Gilbert says, "Yes, yes, I am."
"Then would you scratch my nose?"

Next there is Mrs. Alfred, who asks about
Her husband down the hall, "Is he warm enough?"
"It's Alzheimer's, you know." She likes reports
And always sends a note propped by his cup,
Knowing he will fold the note repeatedly,
Tuck it away, take it out, try to read.

Twice now Mrs. Gilbert's wing has telescoped
As though her head were driven back,
Twice the ceiling, walls, and floor contracted
To a half light, then widened and returned,

As she leaned even farther forward
In her exaggerated push against the cart.
Both times her parents came to mind, grown small
In their clothes as if they shrank from touch
As if old, though not that yet, tired maybe,
And silent as two sullen absences,
Home late and neither noticing
How cold and dark the house had turned.

Both times her wing tightened to its peep-sight gray,
Mrs. Gilbert paused only briefly,
As though distracted by a name recalled,
Or stalled by something she'd misplaced;
Then, leaning ahead, the back wheels swiveled,
And as she moved her corridor returned to color.

The last room produces Mrs. Clement,
Who propped up in her partially raised bed
Is the best adjusted of them all;
Always with something gracious to say,
She thinks herself a guest in this hotel,
Where she appreciates the service
But occasionally asks for a different room.

With Mrs. Clement and all the rest settled,
And the bronze tinted windows darkening
Toward reflection, Mrs. Gilbert is free
To drive the few blocks home. Sometimes
She stops for something frozen, which she cooks
While listening to the news. After dinner
There are letters, the papers, the news again,
During which Mrs. Gilbert sometimes lists
The names of all the patients on her wing,
Now and for the last five years she's volunteered,
Feeling especially mindful of them now,

Between the two tall holidays,
With all the carols and the visits over
And for the next few quiet days
Little sense of anything ahead.

There's always the artificial tree to pack,
Practical because its needles do not drop,
It will not burn, requires no water,
Is light, and never changes size—
Its ornaments forever adequate . . .
And there are the clocks along the hall,
As round-faced and reassuring
As the watercolor seasons painted
On calendars some patients get by mail.

Limited and quirky as these comforts are,
Mrs. Gilbert finds them preferable
To the new clock radios the hospital
Has given as a present to each room,
All of them off-white, with digital faces
Blocked in crude illuminated reds
That reconfigure without changing place.
To Mrs. Gilbert, this collective gift,
A bargain no doubt, plays, in miniature,
All that Times Square, the hotel parties, Big Bands,
On the competing stations—all that these mean—
Summed up, she supposes, by the Times Square crowd itself.

Although she never waits till twelve,
Saying she cannot keep her eyelids up,
Mrs. Gilbert's not too sure how much she sleeps either,
Hearing in the white noise of the vent
Above her bed a rush of overlapping cries;
Only the air, but sometimes when she's tired
She remembers the man she heard about

232

Who claimed there was a way to play back sounds
Trapped like stilled echoes in rocks, the lava
Of Pompeii, say, the people in confusion,
Calling out and running to no escape.

And sometimes just before she's drifted off,
She hears the static of an old radio,
Her parents' Zenith, audible upstairs
Where she has waited in her bed, half asleep,
Holding out . . . first the background of the crowd,
Then suddenly all one voice and counting down,
As the last few seconds of the year
Widen like drained parentheses.

When she could not sleep without a light,
She too left her radio on for the voices;
She too wrote her husband short careful notes,
Placed beside a photograph or window,
A sentence or a phrase she hoped he'd catch,
Between all the folding and unfolding,
While at home, in bed, there were crosswords to do;
Propped up, her pillows banked a quiet minus,
As she piled their angles into height,
Wondering how deep a sleep could get
Drifting under a few half-completed words.
It was as if she stood dumb in her own name,
Or stilled before the plate glass to a shop
That, lights turned out, darkened and reflecting,
Gave her back a face she'd never seen.

But what she calls the taking down,
The season that she now walks through,
Stretches wide of any one reflection,
Wide even of her bringing water
To the few stalled days remaining

Of the shipped apples, oranges, and pears
Lining the complex sills to every room . . .
And the names, the essential names,
Answer through the hall's suffusing gray
As she feels somehow they always did,
Long before her leaning to the cart's odd wheels,
Or finding in the air's subtractive touch
That each was thirsty and completely recognized.

Blood

Known for its repertory lineages
By which we generalize the who and what,
And for the figures that we make of it,
Bloodline, bloodlust . . . it runs between
The spent asphyxiated blues
Of time and work and that bright filigree
Through which the impounding heart pumps back
Our reddened and ventilated lives—
As if among the wind's announcing leaves
That dryly say the world's deciduous,
We breathed a lasting shape that let us stay.

Scripted in a secret and minute hand
That writes itself and signs its origins
In unrepeated blues and reds,
The blood holds to its systole and diastole,
Flooding and circling rawly on
As rhythmic tides reduplicate their shores,
As opened wounds edge inward, welling,
Fresh surfacing and taken by the air . . .
Till drying to a lake-bed crust of drought,
There where the healing scab prevents the scar,
Blood surfaces our dust, and something more,
The potent changing earth of us.

Buddhist Temple on New Year's Day

Sister Bernetta Quinn, O.S.F.

This is the Year of the Snake.
At the entrance to the enclave of the long dead
Joss sticks burn for today only
Before burial figures, capped and bibbed in red.
What hungry ghost bit into that *mikan*
Placed for love or fear on a moss-green tomb?
Clicking of cameras, of yen against the grates.
The air is spiced with incense,
Sweet with fresh chewing gum.

I stand apart, uneasy, without prayer.

A child in stiff cerise and gold
Trips, and is set upright by laughing parents.
Ignorant of Bethlehem, the families ask for luck.

Making my exit through the worshippers,
"*Konnichi wa,*" I say, "*Omedeto gosaimasu.*"
The pagan sun shines in my Christian eyes.

My Brother's Angel

For Phil Levine

Len Roberts

I carved my brother an angel
    when he came
home from the war, a foot tall,
    with three-inch wings
and a thin halo of wire sticking
    out of his head,
and I set it on his bedroom dresser,
where his pictures of naked women
    used to be hid,
the angel's eyes turned toward him
    where he slept
in his new madness, the angel's
    mouth open
over the many bottles of pills,
the book HOW TO GET WELL, above
    the small flags
of our country he'd glued to
the wooden box that held his medals.
At night, when I shut off my light
    and saw his
still lit across the dark parlor,
I thought the angel would be glowing
    into his bruised
head, I thought the angel must have
    flown
about that small room with the single
    bed

singing songs only my brother could
    have understood
for I would hear him hum
into the darkness until I slept.
    When I woke
my brother was gone to the ninth floor
    of the Veterans Hospital, or
so I was told, but even then I knew
    the Angel
had taken him under his wing and broken
    his mind
even more, and his heart even more,
    so
he might see God and live with Him.
That the Angel had taken my brother
    to the Deepest Pit
of Hell and left him there sure to ascend,
learning the difference between the City
    of the Living
and the City of the Dead, learning the thin,
    black, papery wings
that crackled in his ashen head, the Great
    Dark
that Sister Ann had said we all must see
before we rise into the light, whole and clean
    and finally free.

When the Bishop Came

These angels were messengers
of the Lord, we were told as we sat
in straight pews they had brought
into the classroom because
the Bishop was coming with his ring
and miter, so he could see
who could answer the sacred questions
from the heavenly blue
Baltimore Catechism,
Jimmy Legasse and Joseph McGraw
in front because they were smart,
followed by Gabriella Wells and Irene
Tousignant, their dresses pressed
and hair curled in rolls Donald Wilcox
always put his fingers into, Donald
who stayed after school every day
because he was sloppy, fat, and cursed,
Donald, whose eyes were a quiet gray
even that day Father slammed him
from wall to wall of the yellow
cafeteria, none of us knew
for what. And it was Donald
the Bishop saw, the black sheep
so obvious in that fourth-grade
flock, and it was Donald he asked
the Eight Beatitudes, the Cardinal
Sins, the Apostles, even, finally,
the Pope's name, Donald
who did not get one answer right,
whose flesh turned that translucent
pig-pink with shame or fear or grace
when the Bishop walked down to his last

239

pew in the last row by the window
and put his gem-studded-sparkling
ring out, which Donald held up to the sun
to see sacred streaks of light flash
before he bowed his head and kissed.

Clear January, zero degrees, my last

day in that state's
winter, and I knelt at my father's
    cold stone
the way he knelt in St. Bernard's pews,
    hungover, limp
with the stink of drunk Irene flooding
    him, the jungle
rot holes of his face glistening
in the stained glass light as he breathed
    the incense deeply
and sorted out for the thousandth-
thousandth time, This is wrong, This is right.
    He rose,
a meek, a pardoned sinner,
no more fights in Boney's Bar,
no more hour-long bottles of liquor,
no more horses at Saratoga, throwing
    the stubs
on the heads in front of him, no more
    cursing
the horse, the horse's mother and father,
the gold initials of his ivory cufflinks
flashing as he dropped the crumpled dollar
into the floating basket, his last buck,
he half-whispered, half-sighed, his beer-
    breath clouding
my face, his bloodshot eyes
glinting the pastel light of saints into my eyes,
his bony hand on my shoulder making me lighter
    than I'd ever been, making me rise
beside him in that last pew in the corner
  of the church,

waiting for Maureen Risteau and her mother
    to click
down the aisle in their Sunday best,
both of us praising the Lord when they clicked
    their way back,
statue-white faces and arms, white gloves,
    white hats with black mesh,
pearl necklaces glistening in that early
    Sunday morning light
about their white, white necks.

Adrift

Mark Rozema

He rides west into the Chukchi Sea,
wind in his teeth and eyebrows aching,
west into a sky of ashes, into fog
where all directions draw him only
further in. He finds the skin kayak
like a feather resting lightly
on the water's silken surface,
waiting for a body to lower itself
into the perfect O of its empty seat.

Like the Irish monks who turned
themselves adrift with neither oars
nor sails nor destination, he waits
for the Spirit of the Lord to breathe
on the water. If only he can match
the ocean's terrible patience,
he will be caught up in that breath
swirling and rippling, welling up
as it does from all places at once,
to make all things new.
He will celebrate sacred mass
on the back of a whale,
he will grow sharp as the point
of a narwhal's tusk, then slip
into the presence of God,
where there is no bottom,
there is no shore.

—Sesholik, Alaska, 1989

The Nuns of Vorkuta Prison

In Vorkuta, there are nuns who lie face down
in the shape of the cross, weeping and praying
for the world. They pray and then wait, still
as light, for Christ to meet them as an image
meets itself on glass, shatters the glass,
and is one thing.

The nuns were told to make bricks
but they refused. They were put in straight jackets
and the jackets were soaked to make them shrink.
Still, the nuns would not make bricks.
So they were put on a hill to freeze
in the Siberian wind.

Crystals of frost, like knives,
laced tree limbs as the sun rose
over Vorkuta. The nuns were standing
on the hilltop, simple and mysterious,
transforming the feeble arctic dawn
into a rich and burning light.

The guards would not touch them.
Prisoners crowded around, to share
their warmth. And now the nuns are not told
to make bricks. They are left alone
to lie face down in the shape of the cross,
weeping and praying for the world.

Passing Over: Easter Dawn

Larry Rubin

Near the end we're scared. So swift the rose
Turns purple, velvet dyed in royal pall,
Clouds losing all identity
In the cloak of afterlight, the cowl,
The scowl, of dusk. Caught in glory, I glare
At stars, aware that each somewhere is still
A sun, and I can run into those headlights—
Like the dog I killed once on the highway.
That dog haunts me now, amidst the dunes
Where grass somehow defeats the sand. The waves
Break slower as the night wears on;
The colors flare once more,
                              the risen rose.

Christmas Poem

The ice on your windshield,
The cold lace at your ear—
A wind through your household,
Combing winter's hair—

One ear's hot and one ear's cold.
(Our lady walks naked on the eggshells.)
One foot's cut—the blood's congealed.
(Take the straw from that infant's stall.)

The ice will turn to flakes of pearl,
The lace will split your ear;
The shells adorn the gates of hell—
(But those hands bleed, my dear).

Early Easter

If it sleets at Easter, all the symbols fail.
The sun's a corpse, and dogwood petals fall
In flutes of ice. That sprig of rebirth green
Grows back into a marble grave—what
Can rise beyond congested sieves of sky?

There is, of course, an equinoctial light
That lasts past six—for weather cannot change
The angle of our planetary bones.
Embryos are hidden in the snow—the children
Hunt for frozen shells. Latin bells

Are tolling through the muffled walls.
                                        I've seen
The stones my daughter rolls, on this cold lawn.

Flying to the Body of Christ

Nicholas Samaras

Oh, we are lifted for a little while,
suspended by the earth's metal.
Scarring the globe to make
the beautiful crafts,
building to Paradise,
we use what lays us down
to resist what lays us down.

A break in the cloud-lining.
Faint blue in the distance.
This high, the world is a pin
where no angels dance.
There in the gulf stream floats
Padre Island.
Leaving the weight
of the world's fractured debates,
I have boarded and ascend
to the lack of colour, to the absence
of Fatima and Erasmus,
cruise to the approaching Corpus Christi
and tomorrow's Epiphany.
When we land, we will open our exodus
to the right of the plane.
But in this altitude, theology's
cracked, human voices
grow pure in silence.

We never expected what we built
and, when Paradise comes, we will
not be able to stand it.

Words for Golgotha

I

I harboured salt and shekels and this, too,
was wrong. And heralded in this song
of blueness lies my conviction, the true
regret. That I, devoid of mother, father, should long
for family in the sapphire's stare, a survivor
of the road, the beggar's bet, coins for the conniver.
And sometimes, eating the dust for supper
when I could draw nothing from the purse
of another man. And fortune, I would cup her
starry hands in mine and curse
my life and repent. So be still, you other,
shedder of blood, pray for your brother
and be still. A gold sovereign has been cast
for our lot. There is no time, no need
to cry for the opportunities passed,
the lamentations wrung, these lives that we bleed.
The true man has come, such a man to condemn.
Remember me—I lived to bloom on this wooden flower's stem.

II

Misunderstood, or better, denied
the equal life of any man—
a horse for honest work, its hide
gleaming in the sun, the ovens, crockery and pans
for eating, the simple goods to live by.
But the grey life I met did not meet my eye.
A dagger was my hard tongue

and spoke quite well.
My services were of the dark alley and rung
to the runes of my persuasive spell,
raping riches from men who fared
my way, leaving them a red wound, my calling card.
The end of the game is always death.
I writhe with indignation, stubborn to the end.
Cheated of rightful silks, failing of breath.
Mercy for the merciless! Rebuked by my own kind.
I stretch against the agony, life's last gaspings.
Sinking down into my knees, I feel the heart's claspings.

III

So named, we stand upon predicated hills
of faith in the twilight of God,
in the valley of man where less is all.
Belief is most often blind, I've heard
said. And I, arborescent, still avow
credence to this fact of dying. Now
to lay me down in such shadows,
having found finer shades of light.
Is it wrong to sink down for such blows
against the Empire, a passive fight?
Books may be written, suit-
able. For a tree has taken root.
I bless unto that fledgling love and will shower
it with strength. And these other voices, to commune
with me in my death, my hour.
To be eaten by sacrifice and journey on.
To die for this truth, of the olive branch and leaf.
I pirouette on sticks between a murderer and thief.

Movable Feasts

1

It is not the form. It is the motion in the form. The want of an object to express the flight that is frozen in tree branches, the want of touching the flight that is held in the structure and bones of a sleeping bird.

It is not the stillness of a form. It is the motion within that stillness, the buoyancy of stone. How a mountain range goes flying in the late slant of light.

2

The sustenance of light. The sustenance of clay and bark.
Mustard seeds buried in the sloped garden.

A mountain is the inhabitant of the mountain.
The breathable interaction of itself and itself.

Gravity is only the bed you lie on.
Not what you are.

The sustenance of light.
Clay. Bark.

3

Athos. The name of the mountain. When you see the elevation, do not look at the crest, but at what dwells there, and you will feel the spirit of the mountain. The way a geography expresses the souls that live on it. The way a man can strike a stone with his staff and crack forth water. The way generations of footsteps on the dusty path faintly echo the name. Athos.

Vespers

Night is dark ink and the weight of stillness.
No sound but the shuffling movements of the living.

Three polite taps at the grey slats of the guest door.
Beneath it, the bobbing, red glow of a kerosene lamp

diminishing. The eleventh hour in Byzantium. Outside, the cupped,
faint howl of a wolf beyond the slumbering ravine. I lumber up.

Two shadows to converge downstairs in the tiny room.
Haloed, wooden faces peer out from the soft gloom.

A drawn curtain the colour of dried blood. We rustle
the hundred years of brocade with our cracked voices.

You give me the Psalter to begin and stand next to me,
a column of dark light. I stammer over the language,

aching from sleep, aching from yesterday's climb through
the olive ravine, the green mansion, the parched resting

in the hollow of the jungle. With my rooms back home
and bills arriving, with the modern world in decline, who

are we to stand away and sing? Who are we not to? You,
black elder, with your liver disease neither advancing nor

remitting, living on this mountain-side in sheer bliss without this
century's medicine, harmonise through the serene hour. We chant

to the hour waning, troparia of loss and receipt, joy and sorrow.
I gaze at the bright, burnished faces of paint and ancient light,

my hands trembling to hold the book steady, the black-bearded,
gold side of your face in the candleglow and shadow.

St. Frideswide's Chapel,
Christ Church, Oxford

Luci Shaw

In this ancient place
one section of the fresco
ceiling has been left
to peel, a puzzle, half
the pieces lost. As from
the bottom of a well I stare
up, waiting for revelation.
A raw plaster frowns
from the past, a closed sky, murky
as thunder, traced with

gold shreds—a snatch
of hair, a broken chin line,
wing fragments in red, in blue.
My eyes invent the truth—deepening
pigment, filling in the detail
of hands, feathers, touching up
the face of an angel. But nothing
changes. The terrible inscrutability
endures, deeper than these
groined arches. Tattered

seraphim flash their diminishing
edges, like the chiaroscuro God who,
if we believe Michelangelo, fingered
Adam into being with a single touch—
whose footprints crease the blackness
of Genesaret, whose wing feathers

brush our vaulted heaven, purple
with storm, whose moon
is smudged—a round, glass window,
an eye moving between clouds.

Golden Delicious

Last night's killing frost uncolored
the whole of the Skagit. This afternoon,
hiking the valley, I found
a spread of apple trees gone wild—
the black nets of branches
heavy with gold fruit, frozen
solid enough to last the winter.

If the freeze had held them
in its hand, vise-hard, not let go . . .

But a rogue river of wind, come loose
from the Sound at noon, is thawing
the valley rotten. And all the numbed apples,
going soft inside, are falling, one,
one, one, till the gray ground boils
with bruised gold, and the old orchard's
autumn air is hung with
the winy smell of perishing.

Camping in the Cascades

After four days in the mountains
we have lived most of the world's
history—its passionate storms,
its silences of fog, the exuberant valleys
and ruinous cliffs, and above
the timber line its tundra of small,
pink flowers shivering on short wires,
that remind me of me, shivering
in the kiss of your breath.

Our uncertainty reveals itself
the way a mountain campanella
half-opens its purple mouth, waxy,
mysterious, tracked by a black thread
of ants. If I could be as sure about us
as the politicians seem to be about promises . . .
The truth is: the future lies
in ambush; more waits to happen

like the surprise of thunder,
when Glacier Lake, blue as a peacock
feather, carrying God's gold solar eye,
turns black with wind.

Moon

Margaret D. Smith

It is colder here than on the moon. At least
it is light there.

There is no singer on earth like the moon,
except the owl.

Where the coyote runs, I see the moon
stand off, watching.

Echoes of God come dancing back
from the dark lake.

In the middle of God, the moon.

How can I bear to pass by?
I will stay the night.

Look, the moon is ebbing,
one wave lapping in.

Sometimes it is hard to trust
one's eyes.

If this is the way I should go—
at least the winter moon goes with me.

In a dry season

I took a walk through a silver-green
olive grove. It was evening, and all I wanted
was a eucalyptus with leaves like coins,
copper turned beryl by the air.

A hummingbird sat vibrating on a light
acacia branch, drumming a twig-thin foot against
his emerald head. A daddy longlegs
extricated himself from a mass of ice plants.

Mother ground squirrels in the grove rose bothered
and blinking. Jays with black crests and
shrieking blue backs razzed
one another.

I spoke to them in a provisional
song, keeping the tune as light as a mass
for a Sunday after Easter. I told the jays
how ambulatory they were, branch to branch.

To the ground squirrels I promised
enough eucalyptus nuts in the winter.
To the great grandfather spider I lowered
my voice and hummed an old hymn he remembered.

Of the hummingbird I asked directions
to the tree of coins gone to seed;
with a whirring he brought me wind
of it.

From the slim trunk's base I pulled
fronds, the whitish stems flexing
and breaking, the oil on my hands an incense
for arrangements in a dry season.

Today

William Stafford

The ordinary miracles begin. Somewhere
a signal arrives: "Now," and the rays
come down. A tomorrow has come. Open
your hands, lift them: morning rings
all the doorbells; porches are cells for prayer.
Religion has touched your throat. Not the same now,
you could close your eyes and go on full of light.

And it's already begun, the chord
that will shiver glass, the song full of time
bending above us. Outside, a sign:
a bird intervenes; the wings tell the air,
"Be warm." No one is out there, but a giant
has passed through town, widening streets, touching
the ground, shouldering away the stars.

Being Sorry

When I was a kid I wanted to drop
a long receiver deep in the sky
and keep on talking farther and farther
till someone understood. I would even say
those three little dots at the end that meant
whatever the listener wants it to mean—the rest
of my life, apologies, denials, prayers.
(With weeping linemen on their poles listening
in and being afraid that I'd stop.) I would stop . . .
and the world would be sorry it had neglected me,
and whatever was in those three little dots at the end.

At Summer Camp

Someone is leaving—tears. Someone
is going away: in all the rest of history
the things that would happen here are changed.
You lift an arm and wave: it would not
be appropriate to fall on your knees and pray.

You have learned to stand wherever
your kind are parting, and slowly
to raise your hand, then turn with only
a slight—an almost unseen—hesitation
and a glance back as you go away.

No one will know, in all the success,
the publicity and praise, that your thoughts
ran under the fence and followed the car
taking a lost one home, past the trees
and the lake and all you wanted to say.

Listening at Little Lake Elkhart

What signal brought us, leaving our work, our homes,
following the faintest of trails? Was there a treasure
that our time has obscured? Is there bread for this hunger,
this long exile from earth our great mother?
Listening as well as we can, we hear the loon cry—
from a dark shore it echoes; it tells how far
the northland goes, one gray lake
then another all the way to the edge of the wind.

Bitter, this land; even in summer it grudges
the sun. Ice fingers the lake edge; rain spits
a few flakes of snow. Out there the loon rides
low in those pewter waves, calling and calling.
The world has this voice; it wanders; it is lost
in the night and the stars. It cannot find where to go.

At a Small College

Words jut forward out of the stone:
"Follow me and I will make you
fishers of people." On the great still earth,
suddenly, this once in your life, you find
your place, alone, where hills and fields
can surround silence; and here for an instant
you rest. All purposes wait: the running
after next effort, the hope and regret.

Without asking, you came. Over the years
a succession of days passed, each a mouth
demanding attention. Strong arms
pushed you. Over hills and around corners
the wind carried views toward you and away.
The sky that watches you now arched over.

Darkness floods forward. Soft on the open
playing fields a bell intones
what it can of serenity. In the still night
your life hurries on, a vault with a jewel
hidden inside. Enveloped by your times,
you stare ahead along the dark road.
You remember to breathe, to stand on the earth again.

Beginning with *and*

Alberta Turner

And you feel a vague lump in your throat, a need
to swallow twice; so you look along your shelf
and see a rind of cheese and a cough drop, stuck.
Through the window a flat moon, more flag than face.
Your throat begins to ache. Perhaps you should
have chosen the fat god, the one that burps,
not the tubercular one with the hollow cheeks.

Once you could pretend a party and pat
sand into muffin tins and sugar the tops,
or pretend equal legs on a forked stick
and gallop it to the barn and neigh.
And once when the sky was tall and the wind still,
you walked through yellow birches into a room
and claimed it for your own, but you never went back.

And you didn't buy a gun nor even find one;
it always stood in the hall among the boots.
But now you lift and sight down the long
barrel till the front and rear sights fuse
and you see a field of gibbets and a field of crosses
leaning toward each other, and you see a child
offer cheese to a dead mouse. And you see
a woman knife herself and a man burn
himself alive because they think they've let
the world become. And as you look, you fill
with a queer joy that ill and good can sing
from the same throat, that the lame can limp

and the sad can laugh and the dead can die,
and you stand and look—and look—
till the gun grows heavy and you lay it down.

Trying to Be Human

In the night a voice mutters and repeats,
Onions hang from the rafters, bread keeps the oven warm,
broom's tied; but in the night that voice.
Is it praise? Is it prayer?
The chimney doesn't know, trees nod.
Is it now? Is it here?

I'm trying to be born:
They topple and toss me,
each takes one end and shakes out the middle.
"Breathe," they curdle. "Breathe,"
and believe I can.

"We know all about fear," the roof says. "We've been
heaped, nailed. Rain drills us, wind lifts
our skirts, ropes thrown over us are weighted
with stones at both ends. And fear underneath:
pressings of cows, squeezings of sheep; ashes
and parings and husks; women and men
in parentheses, their hatch under quilts."

A bread crumb calls, "Look out," a lamp post
makes sucking noises under its cleats, a chair
with arms and lap and no neck mutters
between its legs, "You look human to me."

Wanting a god so much I'd take anything
with shoulders and sleeves, anything single
in the middle and paired on both sides,
returning to itself, born of its own loam,
because anything I lay on air

fluffs, flakes, and follows me down,
because wheels of snow hesitate
and follow me down.

Haydn's Creation:
Ardmore Presbyterian Church, 1978

Jeanne Murray-Walker

Out of the dark we gather to try to make
the world. Removing scarves, we squint at light.
The bass shakes out the wrinkled hills and I
administer the tune to God tonight

so that he will be able to go on
creating fish and fowl. Damage of bells
and damage of the dawn has worn him out.
His voice lies down; his hair grows thin and falls.

The varnish of this floor is worn by paces,
by pressure of prayers and by slow weight of stones.
Here every lucky color drifts to gray.
Here hands that held bright thread relapse to bones.

Yet in the broken edifice of things
where tired angels wear their shawls of dust
contraltos rise again like early sun.
Cellos resolve the morning like a fist

unclenching in the savage presence of
a lover's eyes grown level with desire.
So God, the lover, opens the shut centuries,
shuddering owls and sheep down in fire.

Then all things recognize themselves again.
Giraffes step into bodies, stretch and pause.

Monkeys, hand over hand, learn their own ways.
Field mice balance the moon in tactful paws

till first days break back to the end of time
and man once more in pain puts on his skin.
Astonished knuckles bruise the air again;
snuggle of arteries pumps the wild blood in.

And we break out, rounding a curve of air,
plunging ahead of tempo, O sweet tune.
The light curls through the latticework of stone,
dawns on the angels' wooden cheeks. Is gone.

Directions for Spring

For Helen deVette

Watch the daffodils. Though they are not up yet,
already they are unstable, their high yellow
waving by the deep riverbed like a gang of suns.

Beware of how you plant them. Place the side marked
MADE IN HOLLAND down. Burn the box. Dig holes
at night and do not admit hope to your neighbors.

In winter, do not read Wordsworth, whose fields
permit riots of heat in the most implacable freeze,
whose breeze never stops shuffling pages of stamens.

Do not think of them in the dark, in basements,
while scanning the *New York Times* on the rise of crime,
or while making necessary arrangements with people.

Daffodils will take advantage. If one of them gets her green foot
into your last permanent room, nothing can follow but
bliss, crouching on every threshold, blocking all exits.

Should the strong arms of daffodils succeed in their terrible shove,
you will lose your last method of knowing sorrow:
you will recognize only love.

The End Is Whatever Happened Last

I.

What if I told you that the boy
whose thumb bled for three years
comes to the end of suffering
as one does sometimes, driving along,
thinking of appointments,
of pot roast and potatoes for supper,
ignoring signs, and then the road stops,
abruptly chopped off in a weed patch,
the windshield full of a gray slag pile
covered with Queen Anne's lace.
Trembling, he turns off the motor
and listens while cardinals tie
bright loops, while sunlight
pours down like water and he can move
his thumb and he is absolved
of pain, his heart idling in his chest
like a fine motor after a tune-up.

II.

Meanwhile the heiress who almost starved herself
to death, having receded into her bones,
her wrists dwindling to zeros,
finds the bottom, touches down, and rises
to herself alone in her room at dusk,
disappointed to be looking out of her own eyes
at pulled shades. The bed is firm beneath her,
the cook, gone for the evening,

275

her own young body stuck to the stubborn world,
like an old refrigerator no one can lift.
Everything stands still as an indrawn breath
except the cat, rocking its tongue
down its glossy side, slow righteous strokes
over its haunches, lapping up the vitamin
its own body has secreted. This cat is
the first thing she has ever seen. This cat
is straight from the hand of God. She watches,
learning how to feed herself with love.

Here and at Every Door

T. H. S. Wallace

1—What We Want

A god we can lay our hands on
and lead where we want, a god we
can try and denounce, taking him

up and nailing him down. One we
can bury for the people's good,
the nation, the old state of

affairs, the dark seed of untold
but familiar generations,
olives heavy, ripe for the picking,

our bread unleavened as ever,
Death's blue-eyed messenger checking
for lamb's blood here and at every door.

2—Thoughts of Anywhere but Here

The courtyard fires burn. The guards
and their women huddle in the night
trading long gazes into the flames,

for thoughts of anywhere but here.
I've come as far as brash talk can
carry me. My heart pounds its prison

of ribs, pounds with all the anger
typical of fear, pounds as I
pass myself off as usual.

What can I say? What can I say?
I'm no one! Absolutely not
his friend! I swear by God, not his!

I step beyond the fire's circle,
the gasp and crackle of wood, of dung.
Me with the face that everyone

takes at face value, with a tongue
loose as a lie in my mouth,
hoarse from repeated betrayal.

3—Children of Famine
   John 19:38-42

I am innocent of nothing,
a true bystander, frail man making
small with himself.

I would sooner choose death now than
think of life, weary of reasons,
ears that hear nothing

more than the heartbeating night.
I who refused to accept the insult
of silence, I've

wasted my life on glib affirmations,
easy as fraud to believe in.

We left our starved dreams

in that garden, under that bone
sliver of moon. When evil scrapes
its boot soles,

our hands dangle, a desolation
of gesture. Our eyes glaze
under their half

closed lids. We lie in the rag ends
of our days, children of famine
too weak to cry.

4—Bloodfield

He hears the torches behind him,
their sizzle like spit in fire.
He repeats the words to the kiss.

The slow anger of old wounds glows
under his breath, his face ruddy
with its own heat. The stars, cold

and bright, shine like polished silver,
a full moon like a dead man's face
before him. He gasps at the rope's

quick constriction, kicks his legs.
His toes twitch up the dust as he
swings limp in a shallow arc,

a pendulum telling bad time,
a man with no good memories,
with nothing to speak of.

5—Sleepers of the Most Common Sort

The sparrows scatter and gather
again quite without parable.
Men and women with no future,

we huddle in that room
above the road to tomorrow.
No one speaks, the restless city

beyond our silence tense as an adder.
We hear whispers shiver down
the spine of wind. We tug

ourselves about us for warmth,
but find nothing familiar.
We study our empty hands—

each callous—each gesture
a shrug. The bread on our table
hardens to stone.

How the All-American Dreamwalker Comes Home to the City of God

You meet a man like John, black
as a hole in space, with a look
that pulls everyone in. He stands
like the day and the hour, words
under his tongue, revelation
under his words.

He opens the long abandoned
City of God, insubstantial
walls never meant for defense,
streets yellow with accumulated dust,
trackless as God. Yes. Sapphire
and crystal transpire.

You touch the world's dangerous parts—
skull, scrotum, blood, and breast.
Only now you notice how
the planets align to no
significance, how stars move
in their relative ways.

How you wander like one dream
inside of another, neither of them
adequate! You wake to the canyons
of shadows and everyday lives,
the accumulated litter of men
and women cloaked in steam and rags,

and one who stops you
on the avenue to tomorrow,
his plundered body on his hands.

He tells you snow falls to its oblivion
on these dark streets. It covers
nothing, deceives no one.

Icarium Mare

Richard Wilbur

We have heard of the undimmed air
Of the True Earth above us, and how here,
   Shut in our sea-like atmosphere,
We grope like muddled fish. Perhaps from there,

   That fierce lucidity,
Came Icarus' body tumbling, flayed and trenched
   By waxen runnels, to be quenched
Near Samos riding in the actual sea,

   Where Aristarchus first
Rounded the sun in thought; near Patmos, too,
   Where John's bejeweled inward view
Descried an angel in the solar burst.

   The reckoner's instruments,
The saint's geodic skull bowed in his cave—
   Insight and calculation brave
Black distances exorbitant to sense,

   Which in its little shed
Of broken light knows wonders all the same.
   Where else do lifting wings proclaim
The advent of the fire-gapped thunderhead,

   Which swells the streams to grind
What oak and olive grip their roots into,
   Shading us as we name anew
Creatures without which vision would be blind?

This is no outer dark
But a small province haunted by the good,
   Where something may be understood
And where, within the sun's coronal arc,

   We keep our proper range,
Aspiring, with this lesser globe of sight,
   To gather tokens of the light
Not in the bullion, but in the loose change.

Two Riddles from Aldhelm

I.

Once I was water, full of scaly fish,
But now am something else, by Fortune's wish.
Through fiery torment I was made to grow
As white as ashes, or as glinting snow.

II.

Ugly I am, capacious, brazen, round,
And hang between high heaven and the ground,
Seething with billows and aglow with flame.
Thus, as it were, I'm vexed upon two fronts
By both those raging elements at once.
     What's my name?

A Wedding Toast

M.C.H.
C.H.W.
14 July 1971

St. John tells how, at Cana's wedding-feast,
The water-pots poured wine in such amount
That by his sober count
There were a hundred gallons at the least.

It made no earthly sense, unless to show
How whatsoever love elects to bless
Brims to a sweet excess
That can without depletion overflow.

Which is to say that what love sees is true;
That the world's fullness is not made but found.
Life hungers to abound
And pour its plenty out for such as you.

Now, if your loves will lend an ear to mine,
I toast you both, good son and dear new daughter.
May you not lack for water,
And may that water smack of Cana's wine.

The Rule

The oil for extreme unction must be blessed
On Maundy Thursday, so the rule has ruled,
And by the bishop of the diocese.
Does that revolt you? If so, you are free
To squat beneath the deadly manchineel,
That tree of caustic drops and fierce aspersion,
And fancy that you have escaped from mercy.
Things must be done in one way or another.

Advice from the Muse

For T. W. W.

How credible, the room which you evoke:
At the far end, a lamplit writing-desk.
Nearer, the late sun swamps an arabesque
Carpet askew upon a floor of oak,
And makes a cherry table-surface glow,
Upon which lies an open magazine.
Beyond are shelves and pictures, as we know,
Which cannot in the present light be seen.

Bid now a woman enter in a mood
That we, because she brings a bowl of roses
Which, touch by delicate touch, she redisposes,
May think to catch with some exactitude.
And let her, in complacent silence, hear
A squirrel chittering like an unoiled joint
To tell us that a grove of beech lies near.
Have all be plain, but only to a point.

Not that the bearded man who in a rage
Arises ranting from a shadowy chair,
And of whose presence she was unaware,
Should not be fathomed by the final page,
And all his tale, and hers, be measured out
With facts enough, good ground for inference,
No gross unlikelihood or major doubt,
And, at the end, an end to all suspense.

Still, something should escape us, something like
A question one had meant to ask the dead,
The day's heat come and gone in infra-red,

The deep-down jolting nibble of a pike,
Remembered strangers who in picnic dress
Traverse a field and under mottling trees
Enter a midnight of forgetfulness
Rich as our ignorance of the Celebes.

Of motives for some act, propose a few,
Confessing that you can't yourself decide;
Or interpose a witness to provide,
Despite his inclination to be true,
Some fadings of the signal, as it were,
A breath which, drawing closer, may obscure
Mirror or window with a token blur—
That slight uncertainty which makes us sure.

The Gourd Dipper

The gourd figures primarily in the story of Jonah,
when God made a gourd grow so fast that overnight
it created an arbor to shade Jonah and diminish his
grief (Jon. 4: 9-10). The gourd, suggesting Jonah's
reemergence from the whale, has become a symbol
of the Resurrection."
—*A Handbook of Symbols in Christian Art*

Br. Rick Wilson, TOR

"Walk the fallow rows of the south
twenty until you find a gourd
picked ripe and thumped solid,
one that dreams the ways of
the water.

Hollow it out. Scattering the bright,
slick seeds at your feet, carving
deep as your thirst.
Scrape away the lesser pulp
and let the Barlow blade
shape the Earth element.

Now wash off the crust
of soil with your spittle
rubbing the rind
palmwise until it lacquers
smooth; glaze it.

When you string it out
to dry, have it sing
on a leather thong
eddy in wind currents
and gather strong draughts
to it.

And now, seek out still water
slight with silt and cold.
Dip and draw-up
the shards of your reflection
that spill off the lip's edge.
Here you are free to drink deep.
Let it quell the burning
Let it quench to the core

At last, imagine how long
that gourd-dipper took to find you
how many turnings it may take
before the next one rises
nestled in the dirt mattress somewhere,
somewhere out along the twenty.

Compline

"He walks everywhere incognito. And the real
labor is to attend. In fact, to come awake.
Still more, to remain awake."
—C. S. Lewis

The mountains' frayed edges
lose themselves
in weathered burlap

tarnished bronze of the earth's
paten
whose darkness
surrounds the solitary glow
of the votive lights

the friars' canticle walks
across
this boundaried land
searching

for some star
to steer this stillness
home

and nowhere
to shelter
the vernicle of their hands.

October

Charles Wright

The leaves fall from my fingers.
Cornflowers scatter across the field like stars,
$\qquad\qquad\qquad\qquad$ like smoke stars,
By the train tracks, the leaves in a drift

Under the slow clouds
$\qquad\qquad\qquad$ and the nine steps to heaven.
The light falling in great sheets through the trees,
Sheets almost tangible.

The transfiguration will begin like this, I think,
$\qquad\qquad\qquad\qquad\qquad$ breathless,
Quick blade through the trees,
Something with red colors falling away from my hands,

The air beginning to go cold . . .
$\qquad\qquad\qquad\qquad$ And when it does
I'll rise from this tired body, a blood-knot of light,
Ready to take the darkness in.

—Or for the wind to come
And carry me, bone by bone, through the sky,
Its wafer a burn on my tongue,
$\qquad\qquad\qquad\qquad$ its wine deep forgetfulness.

The Monastery at Vršac

We've walked the grounds,
                              inspected the vaults and the old church,
Looked at the icons and carved stalls,

And followed the path to the bishop's grave.

Now we sit in the brandy-colored light of late afternoon
Under the locust trees,
                        attended and small
From the monastery. Two nuns hop back and forth like grackles
Along the path. The light drips from the leaves.

Little signals of dust rise uninterrupted from the road.
The grass drones in its puddle of solitude.

The stillness is awful, as though from the inside of a root . . .

—Time's sluice and the summer rains erode our hearts
                             and carry our lives away.
We hold what we can in our two hands,
Sinking, each year, another inch in the earth . . .

Mercy upon us,
                    we who have learned how to preach but not to pray.

December Journal

God is not offered to the senses,
                              St. Augustine tells us,
The artificer is not his work, but is his art:
Nothing is good if it can be better.
But all these oak trees look fine to me,
                              this Virginia cedar
Is true to its own order
And ghosts a unity beyond its single number.
This morning's hard frost, whose force is nowhere
      absent, is nowhere present.
The undulants cleanse themselves in the riverbed,
The mud-striders persevere,
                              the exceptions provide.

I keep coming back to the visible.
                              I keep coming back
To what it leads me into,
      the hymn in the hymnal,
The object, sequence and consequence.
By being exactly what it is,
It is that other, inviolate self we yearn for,
Itself and more than itself,
                              the word inside the word.
It is the tree and what the tree stands in for, the
      blank,
The far side of the last equation.

———————

Black and brown of December,
                              umber and burnt orange
Under the spoked trees, front yard
Pollocked from edge-feeder to edge run,

Central Virginia beyond the ridgeline spun with
   a back light
Into indefinition,
                 charcoal and tan, damp green . . .

Entangled in the lust of the eye,
              we carry this world with us wherever we go,
Even into the next one:
Abstraction, the highest form, is the highest good:
Everything's beautiful that stays in its due order,
Every existing thing can be praised
                when compared with nothingness.

———————

The seasons roll from my tongue—
Autumn, winter, the *integer vitae* of all that's in vain,
Roll unredeemed.
              Rain falls. The utmost
Humps out to the end of nothing's branch, crooks there like
   an inch-worm,
And fingers the emptiness.
December drips through my nerves,
               a drumming of secondary things
That spells my name right,
            heartbeat
Of slow, steady consonants.
Trash cans weigh up with water beside the curb,
Leaves flatten themselves against the ground
                and take cover.

How are we capable of so much love
             for things that must fall away?
How can we utter our mild retractions and still keep
Our wasting affection for this world?
             Augustine says

296

This is what we desire,
The soul itself instinctively desires it.
                          He's right, of course,
No matter how due and exacting the penance is.
The rain stops, the seasons wheel
Like stars in their bright courses:
                    the cogitation of the wise
Will bind you and take you where you will not want to go.
Mimic the juniper, have mercy.

————————

The tongue cannot live up to the heart:
Raise the eyes of your affection to its affection
And let its equivalents
                ripen in your body.
Love what you don't understand yet, and bring it to you.

From somewhere we never see comes everything that we do
    see.
What is important devolves
                  from the immanence of infinitude
In whatever our hands touch—
The other world is here, just under our fingertips.

While Angels Weep

Ed Zahniser

Sanctus by Benoit: the organ prelude
further swells our summer-swollen air
that ceiling fans strain to separate.
Robeless the minister allows as how
"Angels weep at how we strut on Earth"
and that "Our God rules not

with an iron fist but with such love"
and "We are made in His image" so
"Are not we also loaded with that power?"
A good question, but the service seems
to end without an answer.
We rise slowly from sticky pews,

unconvincing as gods and goddesses.
Stiff knees anticipate the most
our coming benediction. A good word
hopes to hold us one more week
while angels weep, hopes to bolster us
another week while angels weep.

Prayer for a Hope to Share

Forced so long to hope alone
can we find a hope to share
and unreservedly?
We're out of time for throwing half a bone
each to each. Half to care is not to care
at all. The path ahead looms swervingly

what with the cross put at our backs.
How odd to hope on a death
with a long, still longed-for promise of return.
Two thousand years following in tracks
as gossamer as, however holy, spirit breath.
All *is* vapor. Yet I cannot help but yearn

to turn and turn again; to put my face
to that persistent promise.
What fabric lasts without its knowing weaver
to restore these tatters to a former grace
however flawed? Yes, I would miss
the curious comforts of the true believer.

Prayer for Prayer

Solitude so perfect it's not lonely:
grant us, merciful God/dess, this sense
just once of satisfying prayer
—each of us Your one and only
supplicant. We'll bat across the back fence
dark things difficult to share.

We'll need new words. Nothing off-the-shelf
can quite express our urgent need
simply to confess, unburden, and unbind.
Most prayers turn out like talking to oneself
even with the spirit up to speed
and quiet mollifying the mind.

Accept our words and thoughts as psalms
—or merely our most pitiful candle lamp
that quavers toward the author of desire.
Admit their doubt. And more, admit my qualms.
I feel like a monkey creeping into camp
to worry embers from your fire.

Contributors

Founding director of the creative writing program at the College of Charleston, **Paul Allen** has published poems in *Iowa Review, Poetry Northwest, College English, Northwest Review, Laurel Review,* and others. For his M.A. in English from Auburn University his thesis was on Renaissance biblical translation; his thesis of original poems for an M.A. in English from the University of Florida creative writing program was directed by poet and translator John Frederick Nims. Allen's awards for his work include a South Carolina Individual Artist Fellowship in Poetry. He lives with his wife and two children in Charleston, South Carolina.

Tom Andrews has published three books of poems, including *The Brother's Country,* which won the National Poetry Series Competition, and *The Hemophiliac's Motorcycle,* which won the Iowa Poetry Prize from the University of Iowa Press. He is the editor of *On William Stafford: The Worth of Local Things* (University of Michigan Press), and is currently editing a collection of essays on the poetry of Charles Wright. He teaches at Ohio University.

Jackie Bartley grew up in Pittsburgh, Pennsylvania. She earned a B.S. in biology from Clarion University, as well as a B.S. in medical technology from Mercy Hospital School of Medical Technology. She worked in hospital labs around the country for sixteen years until 1988, when she graduated with an M.F.A. in creative writing from Western Michigan University. She now teaches at Hope College. Her poems have appeared in a number of journals including *The Journal of the American Medical Association, West Branch, Outerbridge,* and *The Maryland Poetry Review.*

Jill Peláez Baumgaertner: B.A. Emory '68, M.A. Drake '69, Ph.D. Emory '80; Professor of English, Wheaton College; Fulbright Lectureship in American Literature (Spain) 1990; Goodman Award in Poetry (Thorntree Press, 1989); Honorable Mention, 1991 Roberts Poetry Awards; Rock River Poetry Prize, Honorable Mention, 1993; currently Poetry Editor of *First Things;* Poetry Editor, *The Cresset* 1973–1989; Editor-at-Large, *The Christian Century;* author of *Flannery O'Connor: A Proper Scaring* (Harold Shaw, 1988); author of *Poetry* (Harcourt Brace Jovanovich, 1990); poems in *New Collage Review, The Centennial Review, Visions,* and many others.

Bruce Bawer's poems have appeared in *The Paris Review, Poetry,* and *The Hudson Review.* His first poetry collection is *Coast to Coast* (1993). He reviews books for *The Wall Street Journal* and *The Washington Post* and has published several books, most recently *The Screenplay's the Thing* (1992), *The Aspect of Eternity* (1993), and *A Place at the Table* (1993). "Art and Worship" was animated not only by the remark quoted in the epigraph but by the coincidence that the church Dr. Bawer attends in New York adjoins the Museum of Modern Art.

Wendell Berry is a farmer as well as a writer. A strong identification with the natural world dominates the work of this well-known poet, whose poetry collections include the poetry collection *Farming: A Hand Book, The Broken Ground, Openings,* and others. He has also written novels and many books of essays.

James Bertolino is a widely published writer who lives on Guemes Island, seventy miles north of Seattle. His seven volumes of poetry include *New & Selected Poems* from Carnegie Mellon University Press and *First Credo* from the Quarterly Review of Literature Poetry Series, Princeton University. His new book, *Snail River,* is being published by the Quarterly Review Series in 1994. The narrative poem "How Could I Have Doubted" is from his new manuscript *Singing the Body Holographic.* He has an M.F.A. from Cornell University and has taught writing for twenty-six years—currently at Western Washington University.

Fr. Murray Bodo OFM is a Franciscan priest. He is writer-in-residence at Thomas More College, Crestview Hills, Kentucky, and is the author of eleven books, including *Francis, The Journey and the Dream* and *Clare, A Light in the Garden.* His latest book, *Tales of St. Francis,* was published by St. Anthony Messenger Press in 1992. In 1994 the same press will publish *The Almond Tree Speaks, New and Selected Poems and Meditations, 1974-1994.*

Scott Cairns was born in Tacoma, Washington in 1954, educated at Western Washington University, Hollins College, Bowling Green State University, and University of Utah. His books include *Figures for the Ghost* (U. of Georgia Press, 1994), *The Translation of Babel* (U. of Georgia Press, 1990), and *The Theology of Doubt* (Cleveland St. U. Poetry Center, 1985). His poems have appeared in *The New Republic, The Atlantic Monthly, The Paris Review, Denver Quarterly, The Journal,* etc. He is currently director of creative writing at University of North Texas, where he is series editor for the Vassar Miller Prize in Poetry. He is an ordained elder in the Presbyterian Church, U.S.A.

Turner Cassity was born in Jackson, Mississippi, in 1929. He attended Millsaps College, Stanford University, and Columbia University before receiving his education in the U.S. Army and the South African Civil Service. He worked at Emory University Library from 1962 until 1991. His most recent collection is *Between the Chains* (1991), published by the University of Chicago Press.

Kelly Cherry is the author of fourteen books, recently including *God's Loud Hand* and *Natural Theology* (poems, Louisiana State University Press), *The Exiled Heart: A Meditative Autobiography* (Louisiana State University Press), *My Life and Dr. Joyce Brothers* (stories, Algonquin Books), and *Benjamin John* (poems, March Street Press). Her translation of *Octavia* will be included in *Seneca: The Tragedies, Vol. II* (Johns Hopkins University Press). Her short fiction has been represented in *Best American Short Stories, The Pushcart Prize,* and *The O. Henry Awards.* She received the first Fellowship of Southern Writers Poetry Award (the Hanes Prize), in recognition of a body of work.

Michael Chitwood is the product of in-breeding and busthead moonshine from the foothills of the Blue Ridge Mountains in Virginia. He has published in *Antioch Review, Threepenny Review, Ohio Review, Poetry, Shenandoah,* and others. His book, *Salt Works,* was published by Ohio Review Books in 1992.

Paul Christensen is the author of three books of prose and four books of poetry. Among his most recent works are *Mind the Underworld* (Black Sparrow, 1991) and *Weights and Measures* (University Editions, 1985). He teaches modern literature at Texas A&M University and lives part of each year in southern France.

David Citino is a Professor of English and Creative Writing at Ohio State. He graduated from Ohio University and received the M.A. and Ph.D. from Ohio State. Among his honors and awards are a Poetry Fellowship from the NEA, a Book Award for Poetry and the first annual Poetry Award from the Ohioana Library Association, a Major Fellowship from the Ohio Arts Council, and the Alumni Distinguished Teaching Award from Ohio State. Citino is the author of seven books of poetry, most recently *The House of Memory* and *The Discipline: New and Selected Poems, 1980–1992.*

Peter Cooley is a professor of creative writing at Tulane University in New Orleans, where he has lived for the past seventeen years. A convert to the Episcopal Church, he was not brought up with any formal religion. He is the author of six books of poetry, the most recent of which is *The Astonished Hours* (Carnegie Mellon, 1992), and his poems have appeared in *The Atlantic, The New Yorker, Poetry,* and other magazines. He lives with his wife and three children in New Orleans. His manuscript in progress is called *Sacred Conversations.*

Robert Cooper is an Episcopal priest and currently Executive Director of the Samaritan Counseling Center in Clearwater, Florida. He is the Poetry Editor of the Anglican Theological Review and the author of numerous poems which have appeared in a variety of journals and magazines.

Robert Cording's many publications include the books *What Binds Us to This World* (Copper Beech) and *Life-List* (Ohio State University Press.) *Life-List* was the winner of the first Ohio State University Press/The Journal award. He received an NEA Poetry fellowship and a fellowship from the Connecticut Arts Commission for Poetry. He was poet-in-residence at The First Place in 1992. "Prayer" is from a recently completed manuscript, *Heavy Grace.*

David Craig is an Assistant Professor of English at the Franciscan University of Steubenville, where he edits a Christian poetry chapbook series. His published work includes *The Sandaled Foot, Peter Maurin and Other Poems* (Cleveland State University Poetry Center), and *Only One Face* (White Eagle Coffee Store Press). (The poems included here are based on *St. Therese of Lisieux, Her Last Conversations,* ICS Publications, Washington, D.C.)

Linda Craig studied at Cleveland State University with Alberta Turner and Leonard Trawick. She also spent some time in the Creative Writing Program at San Francisco State University. Her poems have appeared in *Whiskey Island Quarterly* and *Dark Tower,* and she now lives "in a little music box with her husband and baby son in Steubenville, Ohio."

Peter Davison was born in New York and raised in Colorado. From 1956 to 1985 he edited books for the Atlantic Monthly Press and now does so for his own imprint at Houghton Mifflin Company. He is poetry editor for *The Atlantic.* He won the Yale Series of Younger Poets Award (1963) and a literary award from the National Institute of Arts and Letters (1972.) In addition to nine books of poetry, he has written a "personal history," *Half Remembered* (1973, revised 1991) and a book of essays on poetry, *One of the Dangerous Trades* (1991). He is now writing *The Fading Smile,* a book of biography, autobiography, and criticism about poetry in Boston in the late 1950s.

Stuart Dybek was raised in a Polish-American family on Chicago's South Side. He was educated at Loyola University and the University of Iowa. His books include *Brass Knuckles,* a collection of poems, and two collections of stories—*Childhood and Other Neighborhoods* and *The Coast of Chicago*. Mr. Dybek's work has been widely anthologized, and he has won numerous awards, among them an NEA Fellowship, a Guggenheim Fellowship, and a Whiting Writers Award.

Louise Erdrich draws her characters for novels and short stories from her experiences around the Turtle Mountain Reservation. Her first novel, *Love Medicine*, won both the National Book Critics Circle Award and the American Academy of Arts and Letters Prize. In 1986 she published *The Beet Queen;* in 1988, *Tracks;* in 1991, *The Crown of Columbus;* in 1994, *The Bingo Palace. Jacklight*, a book of poems presented as dramatic monologues, appeared in 1984. Erdrich's popular poems and stories about Native Americans are widely anthologized and translated.

Sybil Estess was born in Mississippi in 1942. She holds a B.A. from Baylor University, an M.A. from the University of Kentucky, and a Ph.D. from Syracuse University. She currently lives in Houston with her husband and son, and has taught writing and literature courses at colleges and universities in Houston. She is co-editor of *Elizabeth Bishop and Her Art* and the author of *Seeing the Desert Green* (poems). Her poems have appeared in *Southern Poetry Review, Shenandoah, The New Republic,* and elsewhere, including *New Texas '91*.

Robert A. Fink is a Professor of English at Hardin-Simmons University, Abilene, Texas, where he directs the creative writing workshops. *The Ghostly Hitchhiker* was published in Corona Publishing's (San Antonio) poetry series in 1989. Fink has recently completed a poetry book manuscript, *The Tongues of Men and of Angels*, which includes a section of persona poems spoken by the apostle Paul.

John Finlay (1941–1991) was the author of four chapbooks of poetry, including *The Wide Porch and Other Poems* (R. L. Barth Press, 1984), *Between the Gulfs* (Barth, 1986), *The Salt of Exposure* (The Cummington Press, 1988), and *A Prayer to the Father* (Blue Heron Press, 1992). His collected poems, *Mind and Blood*, appeared in 1992 with John Daniel Press. Finlay converted to Roman Catholicism in 1980.

Nola Garrett teaches at Edinboro University of Pennsylvania and directs Second Tuesday, the Mercyhurst College Poetry Workshop, Erie, Pennsylvania. Her poems have appeared in *Christian Century, Poetry Northwest,* and *Georgia Review*. Her interests include beekeeping; fast, red cars; gardening; and the stock market.

Dana Gioia, born in Los Angeles, has an M.B.A. from Stanford as well as an M.A. from Harvard. His poems and translations appear in *The New Yorker, Poetry, The Nation, The Hudson Review,* and many other journals. His poetry collections *The Gods of Winter* and *Daily Horoscope* put into practice the controversial poetics he describes in *Can Poetry Matter? Essays on Poetry and American Culture* (Graywolf Press, 1992), a finalist for the NBCC award in criticism. Gioia was a businessman for fifteen years, eventually becoming a Vice President of General Foods. In 1992 he left business to become a full-time writer.

Diane Glancy teaches Native American Literature and Creative Writing at Macalester College in St. Paul, Minnesota. Her second collection of short stories, *Firesticks,* was just published by the University of Oklahoma Press. A collection of essays, *Claiming Breath,* won the 1990 Native American Prose Award from the University of Nebraska Press. Her fourth collection of poems,

Lone Dog's Winter Count, was published by West End Press, Albuquerque. She received her M.F.A. from The University of Iowa.

Jorie Graham has numerous books, including *Hybrids of Ghosts and Plants* and *Erosion* (Princeton University Press) and *The End of Beauty, Erosion*, and *Region of Unlikeness* (Ecco). Her most recent collection is *Materialism* (Ecco, 1993).

James Hoggard (b. 1941), a former NEA fellow, is the author of four collections of poems, two novels, and two collections of translations. Seven of his plays have been produced, including two in New York; and his stories and essays, as well as poems and translations, have been published in several countries. His awards include The Texas Institute of Letters Short Story Award and The Hart Crane and Alice Crane Williams Memorial Fund Prize for poetry. He teaches at Midwestern State University in Wichita Falls, Texas.

Though a Benedictine Oblate, **John R. Holmes** was educated by Franciscans at St. Bonaventure University, where his faith was strengthened by the spirit of St. Francis, and his mind by a B.A. in Journalism (1977) and an M.A. in English (1979). While writing his dissertation on William Blake and Mysticism (Kent State, 1895), convinced that he had given up poetry for scholarly prose, he was stricken by a plague of sonnets on St. Francis, of which "Solvite Templum Hoc" is an example. Holmes has been teaching literature at Franciscan University of Steubenville, Ohio, since 1985. He lives in Steubenville with his wife and three sons.

David Brendan Hopes was born in Akron, Ohio, and is now a Professor of Literature and head of the creative writing program at the University of North Carolina, Asheville. A book of Christian poetry, *The Penitent Magdalene*, appeared from the Franciscan University Press in 1992, and in the same year a Christian mythological novel, *The Book of Songs*, from Dayspring Press. Hopes is a playwright and essayist, who published *A Sense of the Morning* in 1988 and awaits the appearance of a volume of personal essays, *A Childhood in the Milky Way* from David Godine Publishers.

Andrew Hudgins was born at Fort Hood, Texas, and reared on various military bases. He attended Sidney Lanier High and Huntingdon College in Montgomery, Alabama. He has an M.A. from the University of Alabama, course work for a Ph.D. from Syracuse, and an M.F.A. from Iowa. In 1983–84, he was a Stegner fellow at Stanford, and in 1989–90 he was the Alfred Hodder fellow at Princeton. Currently he teaches at the University of Cincinnati. His books are *Saints and Strangers* (1985), *After the Lost War* (1988), and *The Never-ending* (1991).

Jean Janzen was born in Saskatchewan, Canada, in December of 1933, and has ever since squinted into the white glare of holiness. Finding the warmth of earth has been part of her poetic pilgrimage. After 1939 the midwestern United States was home, the plains and endless sky becoming a part of her, and the pumping of windmills an audible search for the water of all waters. Marriage and mothering have been a source of the real, and words for the mysteries lie underneath it all for her, waiting to be found. After child #4 she worked on a masters in creative writing, and now teaches poetry and poetry writing at Fresno Pacific College and Eastern Mennonite College.

Mark Jarman is the author of *North Sea, The Rote Walker, Far and Away, The Black Riviera*, all books of poetry, and *Iris*, a book-length poem. He is a professor of English at Vanderbilt University.

William Jolliff grew up on a farm near Magnetic Springs, Ohio, and now serves as Director of Writing at Messiah College. He and his wife, Brenda, have three children, Jake Henry, Rebecca Peace, and Anna Fulton. His poems have appeared in *Negative Capability, Painted Bride Quarterly, Cutbank, Callapooya Collage, Cincinnati Poetry Review,* and other literary journals.

Barbara Jordan's first book, *Channel* (Beacon 1990), received the Barnard New Women Poets' Prize. Her poems have been published in *Paris Review, New Yorker, Atlantic Monthly, Yankee,* and other magazines. She has received poetry fellowships from the Massachusetts Artists' Foundation and the National Endowment for the Arts. She is now teaching at the University of Rochester and working on a second collection of poetry.

X. J. Kennedy has written or edited scores of books, including teaching anthologies as well as poetry collections. He's also written many rousing children's poems in his *Brats* books. Some of his most recent collections include *Dark Horses* (1992, Johns Hopkins) and *The Beasts of Bethlehem* (1992, Macmillan).

Jane Kenyon was born in Ann Arbor, Michigan, in 1947. She received her B.A. and M.A. degrees from the university there. Her books, *The Boat of Quiet Hours, Let Evening Come,* and *Constance,* were published by Graywolf Press. She is a Guggenheim Fellow, and a fellow of the National Endowment for the Arts. She has published widely in magazines. She lives with her husband, Donald Hall, in rural New Hampshire.

Leonard Kress was born in Toledo, Ohio, and grew up in and around Philadelphia. He has studied religion at Temple University, Polish literature at the Jagiellonian University in Krakow, Poland, and Writing at Columbia. Poetry, prose, and translations have appeared in *American Poetry Review, New Letters, Missouri Review,* and *Quarterly West.* His most recent collection of poetry is *The Centralia Mine Fire,* 1987. He teaches writing at Temple University and the University of the Arts.

Peter LaSalle grew up in Rhode Island, graduated from Harvard, and currently divides his time between Austin, Texas, where he teaches at the University of Texas, and Narragansett, Rhode Island. He is the author of a novel, *Strange Sunlight,* and a story collection, *The Graves of Famous Writers.* He has contributed stories, poems, and essays to *The Nation, Commonweal, Esquire, Raritan, Antioch Review, Massachusetts Review, Virginia Quarterly Review, Best American Short Stories, Prize Stories: The O. Henry Awards,* and elsewhere.

Sydney Lea's five poetry books include *Prayer for the Little City* (Scribner 1991) and *The Blainville Testament* (Story Line, 1992). He has written a novel, *A Place in Mind* (Scribner, 1989), and edited *The Burdens of Formality,* essays on the verse of Anthony Hecht (Georgia, 1990). Recipient of Guggenheim, Rockefeller, and Fulbright fellowships, he funded and for thirteen years edited *New England Review,* now sponsored by Middlebury College, where he taught for a decade. Lea has also taught at Dartmouth and Yale, and is currently on the graduate faculty in writing at Vermont College. He lives with his wife, Robin Barone, a lawyer, and five children in Newbury, Vermont. A book of naturalist essays is forthcoming this year.

J. T. Ledbetter lives in Thousand Oaks, California, but he can still get away from houses and hike in the barrancas with his dog, he says, and pretend timber is still there, as indeed it is, in his memories of southern Illinois, where he comes from. He teaches English at California Lutheran University and finds Robert Frost, William Faulkner, and Thomas Merton good influences as he writes his own poems and tries to help his students find their voices, whether it be in some faraway timber or in the noise of the city. Recent publications include *Negative Capability, Nimrod*, and *Bakunin*.

Denise Levertov, born in England, has lived in the U.S. for many years and has published many books, most of them with New Directions. She teaches each winter quarter at Stanford University; the rest of the year her home is in Seattle, Washington. Her most recent books (1992) are *Evening Train* (poems) and *New and Selected Essays*.

Bob Lietz is currently teaching at Ohio Northern University. His many journal publications include *Antioch Review, Epoch, Georgia Review, Massachusetts Review, Poetry, Shenandoah*, and others. His books are *Running in Place, At Park and East Division, The Lindbergh Half Century, Inheritance*, and *Dangerous Light*. A new collection, *Storm Service*, is currently due to be published by Bas Fal Books. His collection of old fountain pens is the basis of his current project, a book in which he creates lives for the people who owned them. It will be called *Character in the Works—20th C. Lives*.

Marjorie Maddox, an Assistant Professor of Literature and Writing at Lock Haven University, studied with A.R. Ammons, Robert Morgan, Phyllis Janowitz, and Ken McClane at Cornell, where she received the Sage Graduate Fellowship in Creative Writing. She has over 140 poems published in such places as *Poetry, Wisconsin Review, Prairie Schooner*, etc. Her fiction has appeared in *The Sonora Review* and *Great Stream Review*. She has two chapbooks: *Nightrider to Edinburgh (Amelia*, 1986) and *How to Fit God into a Poem (Painted Bride*, 1994). In 1988 she was awarded Cornell's $500 Chasen Award for a sequence of poems; in 1989, the Academy of American Poets Prize.

Paul Mariani's publications are many and varied. He has books on Gerard Manley Hopkins, William Carlos Williams, John Berryman, and Robert Lowell, as well as collections of essays on poetics and a number of poetry books. His poetry collections include *Timing Devices* and *Prime Mover*. His *Salvage Operations* (Norton, 1990) contains selections from these and other books.

Janet McCann has had poems in a wide variety of popular and scholarly journals, including *Christian Century, McCall's, Southern Poetry Review*, and *America*, as well as in four chapbooks. She coauthored a textbook, *Creative and Critical Thinking* (Houghton Mifflin) and received a National Endowment for the Arts grant for her poetry in 1989. She and her husband, philosopher Hugh McCann, have four children.

Howard McCord is the author of twenty-six books of poetry, fiction, and criticism. Among his many honors are two Fellowships from the NEA, two Fellowships from the Ohio Arts Council, and the 1990 Ohioana Award for poetry, The Golden Nugget Award from the University of Texas at El Paso, a Scholarly Achievement Award from Bowling Green State University, a Research Fellowship to Iceland, a Fullbright Award to India, the E. O. Holland Fellowship, and a National Woodrow Wilson Fellowship.

Walter McDonald's recent books of poems include *Night Landings* (HarperCollins), *All that Matters* (Texas Tech University Press), and *After the Noise of Saigon* (University of Massachusetts Press). Other poems have been in *The Atlantic, The Nation, The New York Review of Books, The Paris Review*, and *Poetry*. He is currently Paul Whitfield Horn Professor of English and Poet-in-Residence at Texas Tech University.

David Middleton (born 1949) is poet-in-residence at Nicholls State University in Thibodeaux, Louisiana, and poetry editor for *The Classical Outlook*. His collections of verse include *Reliquiae* (R. L. Barth Press, 1983), *Under the Linden Tree* (Barth, 1985), *The Burning Fields* (LSU Press, 1991), and *As Far As Light Remains* (The Cummington Press, 1993). Middleton joined the Episcopal Church in 1986 and considers himself an orthodox Anglican traditionalist.

Born and raised in New England, **Raymond Oliver** married Mary Ann McPherson of Mobile, Alabama, has two grown children, and has lived in the San Francisco Bay area most of his life. A convert to Anglicanism and a Professor of English at U.C. Berkeley, he specializes in poetry and Anglo-Saxon studies. He is linguistically and literarily fluent in French, English, and German. His main publications in poetry are *To Be Plain* (1981), *Entries* (1982), and *Beowulf: A Likeness* (1990). He is convinced that strict metrical poetry is language at its most focussed and most intense.

Molly Peacock is the author of three books of poems, *Take Heart* (Random House, 1989), *Raw Heaven* (Random House, 1984), and *And Live Apart* (University of Missouri Press, 1980.) Her poems have appeared in the leading literary magazines and in journals such as *The New Yorker*, *The Nation*, *Paris Review*, and *Poetry*. She is president of the Poetry Society of America and has been a Visiting Professor at a number of universities, including N.Y.U., Barnard, Columbia, Sarah Lawrence, and Bucknell. Her maternal grandmother sent her to the La Grange Baptist Church vacation Bible school every summer as a child. There she became interested in how strange it was to pray (she felt she'd never learn how), did camp crafts, and looked out the window into the farmlands that stretched in every direction from the country church. This is the source of "Prairie Prayer." As an adult she became an Episcopalian.

A Connecticut native, **Marjorie Power** received a B.A. in English from San Francisco State University in 1969. Since then, she has lived in the Puget Sound area. She is married and has a twenty-year old son who is full of mirth. Her poems have appeared in one full length collection— *Living with It*, Wampeter Press—and in seventy-five other publications.

Wyatt Prunty has written a book on historical poetics, *"Fallen from the Symboled World": Precedents for the New Formalism*, as well as numerous poetry collections. The poetry books, published by Johns Hopkins, include *Balance As Belief; What Women Know, What Men Believe;* and *The Times Between*. His most recent book is *The Run of the House* (1993).

A Franciscan from Rochester, Minnesota, **Sister Bernetta Quinn, O.S.F.** is known for her study, *Metamorphosis in Modern Poetry*, and her collection of lyrics, *Dancing in Stillness*. Pound and Stevens are the subjects of her scholarship. One year's teaching in Tokyo led to the poem included here. The Gordian Press hopes to publish more of her work.

Len Roberts is the author of five books of poetry, one of which, *Black Wings*, was selected for the National Poetry Series, 1989. His fifth collection, *Dangerous Angels*, was published by Copper Beech Press in Spring, 1993. In July 1992, Silverfish Review published his chapbook of poems, *Learning about the Heart*, winner of Silverfish's annual competition. Roberts has received a Guggenheim Fellowship in Poetry (1990–1991) and two National Endowment for the Arts Awards in Poetry (1984, 1989) in addition to other awards. He was a Fulbright Scholar to Hungary for the 1988–89 academic year, and a Fulbright translator in spring of 1991. His poems have appeared in *Poetry, The American Poetry Review, The Hudson Review, The Chicago Review, Paris Review,* and others. He lives in Hellertown, Pennsylvania, with his wife and three children.

Mark Rozema says that much of his writing might be called autobiography of spiritual search. He invents stories that really are a way of talking about his own life. Recent fiction of his has appeared in *Literature and Belief,* and nonfiction prose in *Puerto del Sol.* He has worked as a professor of English, commercial fisherman, firefighter, and manager of a group home for developmentally disabled men. Currently he lives in Missoula, Montana, where he is seeking a degree in wildlife biology.

Larry Rubin teaches English at Georgia Tech in Atlanta and has published three books of poems (U. of Nebraska; Harcourt, Brace; and Godine.) His poems have appeared in *The New Yorker, Poetry, Sewanee Review, American Scholar, Yale Review, Harper's Magazine, The Nation,* and other literary journals, as well as in a number of anthologies, including *A Geography of Poets* (Bantam, 1979) and *The Norton Introduction to Poetry* (W. W. Norton, 1986 and 1991). In 1961 he received the Reynolds Lyric award from the Poetry Society of America, and in 1973 their Annual Award.

Nicholas Samaras's first book of poetry, *Hands of the Saddlemaker,* received the Yale Series of Younger Poets Award for 1991 and has been published by Yale University Press. His academic degrees include a Ph.D. from the University of Denver, an M.F.A. from Columbia, an M. Div. from Holy Cross, and a B.A. from Hellenic College. Besides receiving the Yale Younger Poets Award, he has also received the Colorado Center for the Book Award (1992), the New York Foundation for the Arts Poetry Fellowship (1986), and many other awards. His poetry publications include *The New Yorker, The Paris Review, The New Criterion, The American Scholar,* and many other national periodicals. Mr. Samaras has recently given executive permission from Athens, Greece, to translate and publish the writings of the late Greek poet Tasos Leivaditis, whose twenty-two books have not appeared in English.

Luci Shaw, adjunct professor of poetry, New College, Berkeley, and adjunct professor and poet-in-residence, Regent College, Vancouver, has led creative writing workshops across the continent and in England. President of Shaw Publishers and a member of the Chrysostom Society, she is author of five volumes of poetry, including *Polishing the Petoskey Stone,* and editor of three poetry anthologies. Her other books include *God in the Dark, Life Path* (on journal keeping), and *Horizons: Exploring Creation.* Her new book of poetry, *Writing the River,* will be published in May, 1994 by Piñon Press. She lives in California.

Margaret D. Smith has published a book of forty-four sonnets, *A Holy Struggle: Unspoken Thoughts of Hopkins* (Shaw Publishers, 1992) and a book on addressing one's journal to God, *Journal Keeper* (Eerdmans, 1992). She teaches poetry writing and journal keeping to students of all ages. She has two sons and lives in Washington, where there are few dry seasons but many moons.

William Stafford (1914–1993), published many collections of poetry including *Stories That Could Be True, A Glass Face in the Rain, An Oregon Message, Passwords, Smoke's Way,* and *Things That Happen Where There Aren't Any People.* Among his other work is an account of serving as a conscientious objector in World War II, *Down in My Heart.* His poetry and prose from the early 1950s on appeared in *Atlantic, Nation, Poetry, Harper's, Hudson Review, New Yorker, Northwest Review, Yale Review,* etc., and he served as Poetry Consultant for The Library of Congress.

Alberta Turner is Associate Editor of *Field*. Her books of poetry include *Need, Learning to Count, Lid and Spoon,* and *A Belfry of Knees*. She has also edited three teaching anthologies, *50 Contemporary Poets, Poets Teaching,* and *45 Contemporary Poets,* and she has written two textbooks. She currently lives in Oberlin, Ohio, and is Professor Emerita at Cleveland State University.

Jeanne Murray-Walker's poetry is collected in *Stranger Than Fiction* (Quarterly Review of Literature), *Coming into History* (Cleveland State University Poetry Center), *Fugitive Angels* (Dragon Gate), and *Nailing Up the Home Sweet Home* (CSU Poetry Center.) Her poetry has won many prizes and fellowships including five Arts Council grants, the Atlantic Monthly Fellowship at Bread Loaf School of English, an NEA , and The Prairie Schooner Strousse Award. Her plays have been produced in Washington, Boston, and London. She is a Professor of English at the University of Delaware.

T. H. S. Wallace's poems have appeared nationally in *Mid-American Review, Sewanee Review, Southern Poetry Review,* and other journals. His first book of poetry, *Beyond the Neat Houses Cheap Talk Built,* was published by Linwood Publishers in 1988; his second, *Raw on the Bars of Longing,* was published by Rabbit Press in 1994. Wallace received the Sri Chinmoy Prize First Place Award for Spiritual Poetry in both 1983 and 1988 and First Prize in the National Literary Competition on the Convocation of the Church and the Artist, sponsored by the Catholic Diocese of Seattle, Washington, in 1987. T. H. S. Wallace is a member of the Religious Society of Friends (Quakers) and resides in Camp Hill, Pennsylvania, with his wife, Diane.

Richard Wilbur was the nation's second Poet Laureate (1987–88), and his *New and Collected Poems* brought him a second Pulitzer Prize in 1988. Recent books are *More Opposites* (1991) and a translation of Moliere's *School for Husbands* (1992). He has taught at Harvard, Wellesley, Smith, and elsewhere, and besides his more than six books of poetry, he has done translations of Moliere and others, and essays on poetry. He and Lillian Helman collaborated on a comic-opera version of *Candide.*

Br. Rick (Didacus) Wilson, TOR, is a Franciscan Brother who lives in Washington, D.C. Though a former high school teacher, he is presently a Ph.D. candidate and lecturer at The Catholic University of America. He is the author of two collections of poetry, *Off the Back Roads* (Hard Cider Press, 1979) and *Between a Rock and a Heart Place* (Scripta Humanistica, 1987). His poems have appeared in numerous periodicals, including *St. Anthony Messenger, The Other Side, The Rolling Coulter, Poet Lore,* and *Piedmont Literary Review*. He was the recipient of the David Loyd Keeger Literature Award and *Phoebe: The George Mason Literary Review's* Poetry Award in 1976.

Charles Wright was born in 1935 in Pickwick Dam, Hardin County, Tennessee. Some of his awards include a Fulbright Lectureship in 1968–69, two NEA grants, 1974 and 1984, a Guggenheim Fellowship in Poetry, 1975, *Poetry's* Eunice Tietjens Award in 1969, the Melville Cane Award in 1976, the Edgar Allan Poe Award in 1976, an Academy-Institute grant in 1977, and, in 1992, the Medal of Merit Award. In 1979 he was awarded the *Pen* Translation Prize for his work with Montale; in 1983 he was a cowinner of the National Book Award; in 1980, the Ingram Merrill Fellowship; and in 1987, the Citation in poetry by the Brandeis Creative Arts Awards. In 1993, he won the Ruth Lilly Poetry Prize. He teaches at Virginia.

Ed Zahniser lives in Shepherdstown, West Virginia, with his wife, Christine Hope Duewel, and their two sons. These poems are from a cycle that chronicles the worship services of Shepherdstown Presbyterian Church, a small-town congregation. John Berryman made real for him the religious poem in a thoroughly contemporary voice. Zahniser's books of poetry include *The Ultimate Double Play* (1974), *The Way to Heron Mountain* (1986; 1989), *Sheenjek & Denali* (1990), and *A Calendar of Worship & Other Poems* (1994) from Plane Buckt Press.

He has also written books and parts of books on natural history topics. His poems, short fiction, and essays have appeared in many literary magazines, and he also writes a weekly column in the *Shepherdstown Chronicle* and serves as contributing editor for the arts for the *Good News Paper*.